'Vile Florentines'

Timothy Holme

'Vile Florentines'

THE FLORENCE OF DANTE, GIOTTO AND BOCCACCIO

CASSELL
LONDON

CASSELL LTD
35 Red Lion Square, London WC1R 4SG
and at Sydney, Auckland, Toronto, Johannesburg,
an affiliate of
Macmillan Publishing Co., Inc.,
New York

First published 1980

ISBN 0 304 30323 2

Typeset by Inforum Ltd, Portsmouth
Printed in the United States of America

For Bruna and Tullio with love

CONTENTS

'To the most exceedingly vile Florentines within the walls.'

From a letter written by Dante Alighieri to his fellow citizens

PROLOGUE

In the ailing and bloated recluse of Certaldo it was hard to recognise the brilliant young philanderer, Giovanni Boccaccio, author of the outrageous *Decameron*, the most scandalous and widely read book of the century. Indeed, he was hard put to it to recognise himself; and as for *The Decameron*, he had long since dismissed it in horror as the work of 'a squalid pimp, an incestuous ancient, a dirty old man, a foul-mouthed calumniator who sticks his nose into other people's misdeeds'.

Boccaccio had finally retreated to Certaldo — his childhood home, principally noted for its onions — when he was fifty-eight. He wanted no more to do with Florence, the great city. He preferred to be thought of as coming from Certaldo. Indeed, he had always been in two minds about Florence, but now it was altogether damnable in his eyes, governed as it was by low-born ignoramuses. He loathed them, 'the gluttons, the frequenters of taverns, the whoremongers and the other thieving scum' who 'couldn't even count the fingers on their two hands, although they were supreme masters when it came to using them for stealing'.

His life lay about him in ruins. His work he saw as mere literary flotsam and jetsam. He was practically penniless and had been pathetically grateful for the fifty golden florins left him by his dear friend Petrarch to buy himself something fur-lined for the bitter winter nights. Moreover, a prolonged and exacerbated andropause had embittered him. He had no love for the world about him. That magic which had haunted his young manhood had dissipated like a cloud of incense in an icy gale.

And as for the headlong riot of carnality he had indulged in during his youth, what had it led to but the catastrophic mental and physical collapse he was now enduring? He suffered from scabies, breathlessness, constipation, a swollen spleen, atrocious kidney pains and an intermittent but cruelly hacking cough.

'My body is heavy,' he had written to a friend, 'my step unfirm, my hand trembling; the pallor of death is in my face, I have no appetite, everything upsets me. The strength of my soul is failing, my memory almost gone, my genius turned to imbecility.'

He had even allowed the scholarly bachelor solitude he so greatly treasured to be violated. His brother Jacopo had married for the second time, in spite of Boccaccio's warnings, and had now come with wife and two children to live at the family home in Certaldo. Boccaccio had been appalled at the prospect, but had reluctantly given way. 'I am not made of iron,' he had written to a friend. 'Their prayers conquered me.' So now to cap everything else the household peace was shattered by female comings and goings and the dreadful clamour of two little boys.

Sitting alone in his room Boccaccio must have thought much about his own life and the lives of his famous contemporaries and predecessors in Florence. Above all, Dante Alighieri, the author of that *Comedy* on which Boccaccio had had the honour of bestowing the adjective *Divine*.

Boccaccio had worshipped Dante since childhood and had written the first biography of him, interviewing people who had known him, catching vital information before it was irretrievably swept away.

Another famous Florentine Boccaccio had written about was Giotto, the peasant boy from the Mugello valley who had grown up to become the greatest artist of the age, the architect of Florence's stupendous cathedral tower and the tightest-fisted usurer in the city.

Then a little later there had been Petrarch, the uncrowned king of intellectual Europe, the poet whose love-from-afar had brought immortality to a girl called Laura. The same Petrarch whose friendship had been the most signal honour of Boccaccio's mature years.

And many others as well — poets, soldiers, popes, emperors,

artists, courtesans . . . All different, yet all united by the city in whose towering tragi-comedy they had played their parts. A city every bit as deadly as ancient Rome, as lofty as Athens, as uninhibited as Sodom and Gomorrah. A city which outran Venice in pride and was the richest breeding-ground of genius that had been known since the ancient world.

It was the story of that city Boccaccio should have told. Only now it was too late. But he had the journalist's eye for it, the poet's sensibility and just the right dosage of humour and cynicism. And all his life he had been a snapper-up of trifles, considered as well as unconsidered.

Only to tell it you would have to go back a long way . . .

1

PORTENTS

In August of 1264 a comet appeared in the sky above Florence. 'It rose in the east with a great light, its tail glowed till it was half-way across the sky to the west, and it remained visible for three months.' Everybody believed it was a sign of some great event and, years later, Boccaccio was able to write without hesitation what that event was.

For exactly nine months after the appearance of the comet a boy was born who came to be known as Dante. So what could the comet have been if not the announcement of his conception?

And while picking about the city for biographical material, Boccaccio came across yet another supernatural announcement of future greatness. Dante's mother had had a dream during the pregnancy.

'It seemed to the gentlewoman in her sleep,' Boccaccio wrote, 'that she was underneath a very tall laurel in a green meadow near to a sparkling fountain, and here she felt herself delivered of a manchild who, in a very short time, nourishing himself only with the berries which fell from the laurel and the waters of the sparkling fountain, became, it seemed to her, a shepherd and sought to procure the leaves of the tree whose fruit had nourished him. And as he strove to do so, she seemed to see him fall, and when he rose up, she saw he was no longer a man but a peacock. She was so struck by amazement at this that she awoke.'

The interpretation was plain. The berries on which he nourished himself were books of poetry. The waters of the fountain represented philosophy. The rapid transformation into a shepherd predicted how quickly Dante would be able to give intellectual pasture to others. The fall represented a political disaster that was to overtake him, and the peacock, with its angelic feathers and the hundred eyes, was the *Comedy*, Dante's story of his own journey through the three great kingdoms of the after-world: Hell, Purgatory and Paradise.

On top of all that, Dante was born when the sun was in Gemini which he always held himself in after life to be an infallible sign of future greatness.

Perhaps it was as well the stars and omens were propitious, for little else was. On the swarming stage of Florence in the mid-thirteenth century, his father was one of the less important characters, a shady businessman called Alighiero Alighieri. 'One of the mice scuttling about in the flour,' someone called him. He came and went, and what he was about nobody was ever quite certain. He was a money-lender amongst other things, but whatever his transactions they were undistinguished and he was neither rich nor important enough to be caught up in the dangerous world of Florentine political life.

The boy was born to this Alighieri and his wife Bella on 13 May 1265. When he was baptised in the Church of Saint John the Baptist a black bean was thrown into a silver bowl to show that a male child had been added to the population (white beans stood for girls in this rough and ready census of births).

The name given him was Durante, but he became known by the shortened, more affectionate form of Dante. A most appropriate name, Boccaccio said in his biography, for it means 'He who gives'.

The baby Dante's world was circumscribed by the walls of his home. It was a rough, square, wood-and-clay building with a thatched roof, very cold in winter when the ill-fitting wooden shutters or flapping squares of leather did little to keep out the winds and draughts which howled and whistled in through the glassless windows. The grown-ups then went about the house in animal skins and hats. Everybody slept fully dressed in winter and naked in summer.

The floor was covered with straw which quickly rotted and then stank. The walls had one or two tapestries and recesses which served as chairs, for furniture was scarce — mostly tables, benches and chests. These chests were made of oak or walnut, and they contained everything from flour to linen with pepper sprinkled on top to keep away the moths. The kitchen was at the top of the house so that the cooking smells might go out through the roof; more than the other rooms it was stifling in summer and icy in winter when often the tiles on the roof beams were blown off by the strong winds.

In the first winters of his life, Dante lay in the arms of his mother, Bella, by one of the braziers or the open fire. But Florentine women were busy, and she could not give him very much of her time.

Houses were self-contained, with their own wells and their own ovens for making bread, and it was the women who had to draw the water and get up before dawn to bake the bread. They had to trudge down the high steps into the cellar, too, to haul up the wine and the oil. And they were responsible for the animals which included dogs, horses, donkeys, chickens and usually a pig. The only thing they did not have to do was the shopping, for their menfolk trusted them neither with the family purse nor with their own virtue, and only allowed them out to church. But those who were set on losing their virtue managed to do so anyway, often with the help of old crones who went from house to house selling ribbons and buttons and trinkets, and were always glad to carry messages and arrange meetings for a consideration.

The family was not rich by Florentine standards, but nor was it poor enough to be without hangers-on. There were the servants who lived and died in the household, creating, like the animals, an extension of the family circle. Then there were the poor.

No other people in Italy cosseted their poor with such jealous ardour as did the Florentines. This meant that armies of beggars poured into the city, but even that did not diminish the Florentine enthusiasm for charity. According to the chronicler Giovanni Villani, there were, to the 6,000 rich Florentines 'who owned rich and luxurious houses', 17,000 beggars and 4,000 poor people, which was too much even for the numerous hostels and hospitals (with more than a thousand beds exclusively at the service of the poor). Many of these people, then, were looked after by private families, and the Alighieris had their share.

The household rose at dawn and went to bed at sunset, taking one meal in the middle of the morning and another towards the end of the afternoon. Together with servants and destitute guests, the family ate on benches and stools around a low table. People ate in couples, each couple sharing a wooden spoon, a bowl and a crockery cup, making do, for cutlery, with a pocket dagger which, Florence being Florence, might well be used for dispatching a fellow Florentine between meal times. The ladies wiped their mouths on the wide sleeves of their dresses, and bones were thrown under the table to be dealt with by the dogs.

The Florentines were <u>great meat-eaters,</u> consuming particularly mutton and lamb, as the city not only raised its own sheep in the surrounding countryside, but also imported the animals. And although it was held that pigs— which rooted about in the filthy streets — were bearers of leprosy, pork was nevertheless a great delicacy. The meat was often high which explains the use of highly flavoured sauces with garlic and wine. Duck was served stuffed with garlic, rabbit stuffed with carrots. Beans were (and still are) a typical Florentine delicacy, and fish, as a penitential food, was eaten on Saturdays as well as Fridays. For pasta the Florentines consumed large quantities of lasagne.

Drinking was a serious business and went on long after the meal was over. Drunkenness was rampant among women as well as men, and abstemiousness was so rare as to be considered an eccentricity warranting a surname of its own — Bevilacqua or Drinkwater. The demand for wine was so great that, apart from their own massive production, the Florentines had to import from Sardinia, Corsica and Crete.

The routine of Dante's earliest years in these surroundings was peaceful enough, geared to the rhythm of the sun and ordered by the bells of a nearby Benedictine monastery ringing terce and nones. But he cannot have been very old when he first began to hear something of the violence which raged all about his home and which was so soon to catch him up, savagely cutting short his chosen career and leaving him only the possibility of being his naked self.

If one single event could be held responsible for this violence which continued to rack Florence, it was a particularly vicious murder which had occurred just half a century before Dante was born. Though even before that violence had always been a Florentine speciality. The city originally attracted attention to itself for the quality of its gladiators, and one of the earliest Florentines was a slave's son who first went into the arena at the age of nine and never knew defeat until he was killed in Milan at the age of twenty-two, an event which plunged the city into mourning.

The very city founders were men of war — tough Roman legionaries in retirement set to reclaiming the land along the River Arno for agriculture under a special law created by Julius Caesar. And when these retired legionaries came to dedicate the place they made a grim and significant choice of patron in Mars, the god of war. From the earliest days a statue of him was venerated in Florence and until it was finally swept away in a flood towards the end of this story his influence was balefully supreme over the city's destiny.

Not long after the foundation, a small Oriental colony selling ointments laced with spells, love potions and cosmetics began to grow up about the Roman arena. Here, too, lived the flower girls who sold garlands and, if one is to judge by the magnificence of some of their tombs, other things besides. These people were the forerunners of the Florentines whose bawdy doings were to be recorded in Boccaccio's *Decameron*.

The more sober-minded and industrious of the early citizens worked iron, copper, wool and stone, and before long they also began to dye and process wool, at which a big fragment of the Florentine jigsaw puzzle fell into place, for all the enormous wealth that was to grow there was founded on wool.

The Florentines themselves said that Christianity was brought them by Saint Barnabas, Saint Paul's travelling companion, directly appointed to the apostleship by the Holy Ghost. And indeed, he may have passed that way, but the known beginnings of Christianity there were more prosaic.

Greek and Syrian merchants began to bring, along with their wares, strange stories about the communities known as Churches in Antiochia and Ephesus and about the terrible persecutions which the people who formed these Churches were undergoing at the hands of the Emperor Nero and his successors. These stories were swopped during loading and unloading, they circulated among the gladiators and flower girls of dubious morals, they echoed about the temple to the goddess of the Nile, Isis, they lapped at the walls of the inner Roman part of the city.

But they did not reach the inner city for a long while. The pagan gods defended the city against grace. Christianity stayed outside where the first Christian cemetery was started, mainly for Oriental Christians whose travels were unexpectedly and eternally ended on the banks of the Arno.

For two centuries Christianity remained, so to speak, in the suburbs. Within the walls a temple rose to the patronal god, Mars, housing his statue. But then, says Villani, 'when the true faith in Jesus Christ spread in Tuscany and throughout Italy and the whole world, the Florentines removed their idol.'

Being Florentines, however, they wanted to be in with the new without entirely cutting off diplomatic relations with the old. The true faith was the true faith, but Martial aid was not to be despised. So they did not get rid of him entirely; they just carried him outside the city walls and put him at the foot of the bridge over the Arno.

His place as patron was taken by John the Baptist, a polemical and supremely Florentine saint whom the people often betrayed but always venerated. The saint who told the publicans 'Exact no more than that which is appointed you' was an appropriate patron for a city whose life-blood was commerce. '*San Giovanni non vuole inganni*,' says one of their earliest proverbs; 'Saint John wants no cheating' (except that it rhymes in Italian). They put his head on the first florins they coined, and there it stayed for nearly three hundred years until Alessandro de' Medici replaced it with his own.

But the event which made Florence a name to be reckoned with internationally happened in 1055, just eleven years before the Conqueror came to England. In that year the Pope called a council there. The city was thronged with eminent ecclesiastics, and the Florentines — fast learning the way with good potential customers — gave them a magnificent welcome.

The vital highway between France and Rome, however, still avoided Florence, an omission which would have to be remedied if the city was to continue growing. And remedied it was. Abbeys and churches began to spring up on the highways around Florence, rendering them so much safer for travellers that Anselm of Aosta, Archbishop of Canterbury, was able to write of the road via Florence that it was 'not the shortest, but the safest'. From now on the city would be on a main artery, fed by a constant flow of men and goods, wealth and ideas.

But the appalling internal conflict which was to be the incessant accompaniment of the rise to greatness was already fomenting within the city walls, and in 1216 there occurred the event which was to be considered the watershed of the city's history.

On the morning of Easter Sunday in that year a young man, mounted on a white horse and dressed all in white himself, rode over the bridge which spanned the River Arno. He was newly married to a beautiful wife and had good reason to be content.

Over on the city side of the bridge, towards which he was riding, there was the statue of Mars, and when the rider was almost abreast of it a group of men stepped out of hiding to bar his way. One of them knocked him off his horse with a club, and the others closed in swiftly, striking with their daggers and then sawing at his veins. The work was quickly over and they left him, a bloody mangled heap, at the foot of Mars.

For all its gruesomeness, of course, it was only another common-or-garden vendetta killing. But there was nothing common-or-garden about the consequences which were to stem from it.

The young man was a Florentine nobleman called Buondelmonte and he had recently been involved in a quarrel with another family. This quarrel had been eventually patched up, and one of the terms of settlement had been that Buondelmonte should marry his adversary's somewhat plain niece.

There lived in Florence at that time a certain Aldrada Donati who had two exceptionally beautiful daughters, one of whom was in love with Buondelmonte. As he rode through the streets one day, he was accosted by the girl's mother.

Standing on the balcony of her palace she called to him and then showed him the love-sick daughter.

'Who have you promised to take for a wife?' she is quoted as saying, 'I was keeping this one for you.'

'And he, looking upon her, was greatly pleased with her beauty, but replied, "It's too late now." '

She answered that it was not and offered to pay compensation to the other girl's family. This offer together with the girl's beauty convinced Buondelmonte: 'and he took her for his wife, abandoning the other he had sworn to take.'

News of this quickly spread through the city. For the jilted girl's family the insult was unpardonable, and they immediately called a council of their faction which included the most powerful and bellicose clan in Florence, the Uberti. At this council Buondelmonte was condemned to death and his killers were chosen.

If the affair had followed the normal pattern there would have been a more or less lengthy chain of revenge killings followed by some sort of settlement, patched together untidily by one or two marriages. What prevented any such settlement and caused the whole thing to escalate into a series of massacres was the position and character of the two families involved, the Uberti and the Buondelmonte.

They were both powerful, and hostilities had been simmering between them for at least a century. This murder was the excuse they had been waiting for, and the subsequent struggle was marked with all the violence of Fascist–Communist clashes in modern Italy.

Fundamentally, it was a struggle for political power. But long after the jilted girl and the murdered Buondelmonte youth had become no more than an old story there remained a peculiarly personal quality in the hatred which kept the fires of conflict stoked.

Many believed that Mars was taking his revenge on the Florentines for having betrayed him with John the Baptist. As Villani put it, 'Well it appears that the enemy of the human race had power over the Florentines because of their sins through the idol Mars, whom the ancient Florentines worshipped, for it was at the foot of this statue that a foul murder was done from which so much evil had sprung for the city of Florence.'

The opposing factions hardened quickly into political parties, those on the side of the murderers coming to be called Ghibellines, the others Guelfs, names which were already being widely used to define the two outstanding political currents in Italy and which are said to come from two German lords, one named Guelf and the other Gibelin. They were friends, the story goes, but one day, returning from the hunt, they quarrelled over a bitch and became mortal enemies. Their personal division so exactly reflected in miniature the political split among the German lords in general that some sided with Guelf and the rest with Gibelin.

Then, as the second group felt themselves to be the weaker they appealed to the Emperor for aid. And the Guelf side then promptly appealed to the Pope. 'And that is why the Holy See is Guelf and the empire Ghibelline, and all because of a wretched bitch.'

Fundamentally Florence was Guelf, not because of any particular devotion to the Pope (who excommunicated the city on various occasions) but rather because the Florentines' desire for self-aggrandisement made them fear imperial domination above everything else.

Nevertheless, they came dangerously near to falling under it when Frederick II was Holy Roman Emperor. Frederick was anxious at all costs to obtain the good will of Florence which was already a city to be reckoned with on a European scale. And he went about it diplomatically. The Florentines, dogged in their dream of the city, had always refused to pay homage to the Emperor. He dispensed them from doing so. The coining of money was the Emperor's prerogative, but in 1237 the Florentines started to coin large silver florins with the head of the Baptist defiantly on one side and the Florentine lily on the other. Frederick turned a blind eye. It was customary for cities to pay him tribute, but he exacted none from Florence.

All this brought a great deal of water to the Ghibelline (pro-Emperor party) wheel. 'When,' they asked, 'has the city been better off? It's protected, but not subjected. It's safe and independent, respected and free.'

For various reasons 1238 was a bad year for the Florentine Guelfs. 'The sun darkened entirely in the afternoon,' wrote Villani, 'and it stayed dark for several hours, and day became night so that many people, ignorant of the course of the sun and the other planets, marvelled greatly, and with fear and trembling many men and women in Florence, for the alarm they felt at such unheard-of things, returned to penitence and confession. The astrologers said that the eclipse announced the death of Pope Gregory, who died the following year, and the abasement and overclouding of the Church of Rome by the Emperor Frederick and great suffering for all Christians, as then proved true.'

Within Florence the waxing Ghibelline side showed unmistakable signs of its intention to take over the city. Fighting broke out in the streets. The deadly bolts of cross-bows whirred among the high towers which the clans had built for themselves, and fire swept through the little wooden houses.

After a few months of this the Guelf front collapsed altogether and its members fled the city and camped outside the city walls where the Ghibellines sallied out and slaughtered large numbers of them. It was the first time that one side had succeeded in ousting the other, but by no means the last; and the temporarily triumphant Ghibellines set about taking their revenge in a way that was to become monotonous.

'They re-made the city to their liking,' reported Villani, 'and destroyed the thirty-six Guelf strongholds, both towers and palaces.' Worse still they tried to destroy the Church of Saint John because the Guelfs had frequented it 'and all the good people went there on Sunday mornings and held their marriages there.'

They decided to demolish one of the Guelf towers which stuck into the sky like gigantic knitting-needles, making it fall in such a way that it would crash into the church. 'But as God willed, through intercession of the blessed Saint John, the tower which was 120 feet tall, deliberately avoided the holy church when it fell, turning and falling straight into the square, at which all the Florentines were much amazed, and the people were greatly delighted.'

But before long the Guelfs began to gain ground in Florence once more, and then for a long time the balance of power shifted backwards and forwards between the two sides, each taking savage revenges when it was up and the other down. Then in 1266, when Dante was less than a year old, there came a battle which was to decide the issue for good and all.

One army was led by Manfred, the brilliant bastard son of Frederick II. 'Fair he was and fine and of pleasing aspect,' Dante wrote of him some forty years later. The other was led by Charles d'Anjou, brother of the saint-king of France, Louis IX. Charles had been called onto the Italian scene as a result of an alliance between France and Pope Clement IV who wanted to halt Manfred's giddy rise to power. He was 'avid for land, mastery and money', in the words of a contemporary chronicler. He was also a man of few words, grim-faced, muscular with a large nose. 'Hook nose', Dante called him on the same occasion as he described his adversary.

If Manfred won, the imperial-Ghibelline-conservative end of the see-saw in Florence would be up and the progressive Guelf end down. If Charles won, the Guelfs would be well on the road to power.

Manfred and his army were in the city of Benevento when Charles arrived in February 1266. The French army was tired and hungry after the long journey and Charles was advised not to join battle. He ignored the advice. 'The day we have so much longed for has come at last,' he said.

The portents were not propitious for Manfred. As he was arming, the silver eagle on his helmet — symbol of imperial power — snapped off and fell to the ground. 'A sign from God,' he is reported to have said. But not for that would he postpone the battle for which he was impatient.

This impatience proved fatal. The imperial army was defeated and Manfred himself fell in the midst of the heaviest fighting. For three days they searched for his body in vain. It was finally found by a looting mercenary who loaded it on a donkey and went crying, 'Manfred for sale!'

It was taken to Charles's tent. He refused it Christian burial because Manfred had been excommunicated, and so instead it was thrown down at the foot of the bridge of Benevento, and as the army passed by, each man threw a stone on top of it until a cairn had been raised over the mangled remains.

In Florence, the imperial-Ghibelline-conservative end of the see-saw was down for good.

2

STREETS

A tragedy more terrible than all the battles in the world as far as Dante was concerned occurred in his life at about this time, before he was five years old. Bella, his mother and his only certainty, died. And to make matters worse his father hastily re-married. The new wife was a lady named Lapa who came of a good bourgeois Florentine family. She gave him three children including a little girl called Gaetana or Tana for short.

It may have been this change in the family circumstances which started Dante wandering about the streets of Florence, learning for the first time what the great city was like. Everything was public.

Another Florentine chronicler, Dino Compagni — Dante's contemporary and friend — describes 'this noble city in the province of Tuscany' as it was then. It was 'rich and abundant with its imperial river which divides the city almost in half, temperate in climate, shielded from harsh winds, poor in subject peoples, but rich in fruits . . . dreaded and feared rather than loved for its greatness by surrounding states. Its citizens are of exceeding civility and its women most beautiful and finely adorned. Its houses are magnificent, full of many useful arts, more than is the manner in any other Italian city. And for this reason many people come from different countries to see it, not because they are obliged to pass through, but for the excellence of its crafts and its arts, and for the beauty and decoration of the city.'

But it was also dense and compact, suffering badly from overcrowding. Although the original walls had been enlarged and extended over the river, the city was still dangerously cramped with warring factions cooped hugger-mugger on top of each other. Their towers were by now its distinguishing mark. 'From the height of the many towers,' wrote a contemporary, 'it is said that she seemed from a distance the most beautiful and flourishing city that could be found.'

Within the walls, however, it was battered. Dante had to pick his way through the rubble of the great houses which had been destroyed in party conflict. But the first great public building, the Bargello — so called because it was the residence of the Captain of Justice, known as the Bargello — had already been standing for ten years when he was born. And in 1237 all the streets had been paved (unlike those of Rome and Paris), 'as a result of which timely work the city of Florence became cleaner, more beautiful and healthier'.

Only relatively so however. The stink was dreadful. Everybody urinated and excreted in the streets and in the many ruins, while those compelled to do so at home emptied their pots into the street anyway. When Dante was ten, the priest of Saint Laurence appealed to the authorities because the smell in the surrounding streets was keeping people from church.

Nevertheless, what Dante saw in the Florentine streets must have kept him endlessly agog. The city life was a continual drama of extremes — magnificence and misery, love and hate, arrogance and humility, joy and despair — all played out in public. Everywhere there were processions — magnificent, brilliantly-staged processions for the great ones of the earth; sombre, but no less cleverly staged processions for condemned criminals who were led, on foot or in a cart, through the city. Beheadings, burnings and burials alive upside-down with legs kicking frantically in the air: these were all so popular that men due for capital punishment were sometimes imported from other cities to satisfy the public demand for macabre drama.

Weddings, births and funerals were all seized on for their dramatic potential. New-born children, even those half-dead, were thrust from hand to hand with shrieks of delight. The dead were carried through the city for several hours to show how important they had been in life and how much they were mourned in death. And lepers still walked the streets ringing their warning bells.

These streets were appallingly crowded, for they were so narrow you often couldn't even walk two abreast, and the shops with their multi-coloured awnings spilled out onto them. The beggars loped or lay about, displaying their sores or infirmities as strikingly as possible, and when it was market day peasants from the surrounding countryside lumbered into the midst of all this with their carts drawn by oxen. Hens, pigs and dogs rooted about undisturbed in the confusion.

The smells were fruitily distinguished. Apart from the human contribution to them, every house had its own stable which gave off the characteristic smell of hay mixed with urine. There were iron rings on the façades of most buildings to which donkeys and horses could be tied, and clouds of flies swarmed about their dung. Towards the outskirts, streams of stinking liquid flowed out from the tanners' workshops, and the tinted water that poured out of the dyers' wasn't much better. Then there were the smells of burnt horn, animal skins and boiling glue.

Much of the butchers' work was done in the street where the guts of slaughtered beasts were snatched up by the stray cats and dogs. All the rubbish from the houses and shops was swept or thrown into the streets which were only cleaned when the Arno flooded.

Personal cleanliness was little pursued. The only serious washing that went on was at the public baths which were open to men and women on alternate days and never by night.

But no smell or dirt could dampen the high spirits of the Florentines. They doted on games — some of them very arbitrary. In Hazard the players threw three dice, the winner being the person whose combined total of pips came nearest to a number previously agreed on among them. In another game the players each put a coin down and waited for a fly to light on one, so indicating the winner. You could cheat by smearing something sweet on your coin.

Chess was the rage. A Saracen visitor to Florence played three games simultaneously in public, winning two and losing the third.

The city was one huge gambling den, and there were official croupiers with a uniform and pointed black hat, and a superintendent of gambling whose job was to see there was no cheating

— an almost impossible task in Florence. Legally, gambling
was only allowed on holidays, but in practice the Florentines
played every day of the week, and so great was their passion for it
that the guilds, whenever one of their members went out of
town, had him swear that he would abstain from all gambling
during his absence for fear that he would lose guild funds. The
centre of this gaming was the Mercato Vecchio, the Old Market, but it went on everywhere — even in church.

There was a rough and ready form of bowls, and boxing was
popular with no gloves, no quarter and no rules.

Falconry was an aristocratic passion. The former Holy Roman
Emperor, Frederick II, the Stupor Mundi, had written a
589–page book about it, held to be the leading study of natural
history of the age. Dante must have seen parties of lords and
ladies hunting with falcons and watched the peregrine plumb
down like a thunderbolt after her prey, soaring back up into the
sky again if she missed. Ladies in the street and even in church
carried falcons on their shoulders as though the birds were some
exotic form of jewellery.

Dante probably hunted too. Using a bow and arrow and
traps, Florentine boys went after the hares and foxes and par-
tridges which abounded in the hills around the city and could
even be caught immediately outside the city walls.

Tournaments in which violent death frequently played its
part were big social events among the aristocracy, lasting for
days and sometimes months on end, helped along with gargan-
tuan banquets. One such, held to celebrate the marriage of
Boniface of Tuscany and Beatrice of Lorraine, lasted for three
months with wine which was drawn from a well in buckets on
silver chains.

The common people went about it more crudely; they simply
rode into rough lists with clubs and belaboured each other to
death.

The city abounded in eccentrics and larger-than-life characters, for whom the Florentines had a weakness. There was a
certain Ciacco who was famous for his insatiable greed. 'Ciacco
was a banker,' wrote an anonymous chronicler, 'and as a result of
too much eating and drinking had ruined his eyesight so that he
could no longer distinguish the coins, and people avoided him
out of sheer disgust.' But Ciacco cannot have been as bas as all

that, for Boccaccio was able to describe him later as 'a man of such amazing greed as has never been seen before or since who, being unable of his own means to satisfy his gluttony, and being moreover exceedingly well-bred and full of the most delightful and pleasant sayings, devoted himself to frequenting, not so much as a courtier but as a brilliant talker, those who were rich and delighted in a good table; and with these at midday and at suppertime, even though he was not always invited, he would stay very frequently.'

There was also an old lady, well on in her seventies when Dante was a boy, named Cunizza da Romano, who was already a living legend. She was not a Florentine by birth, but had come to live with the noble Florentine family of the Cavalcantis after the death of her brother, Ezzelino, son-in-law of the Emperor Frederick II and 'the cruellest and most feared tyrant that ever was among Christians'.

Writers of the time described Cunizza as 'a daughter of Venus' and 'a great courtesan'; they said that she 'burned with carnal love' and 'used up her life in pleasure'. But perhaps she was best summed up by one who wrote, 'At all ages of her life she was in love, and her love was of such magnanimity that she would have held it great discourtesy to withhold it from any who asked it of her kindly.'

The stories of her affairs were endless, carried throughout Italy and beyond by the troubadours, which is hardly surprising when one considers that the most famous story of them all concerns precisely a troubadour.

Ezzelino, Lord of Padua and Imperial Vicar for his father-in-law, had arranged a political marriage for his sister with a certain Count Richard of St Boniface near Verona, but when Richard remained hostile in spite of the marriage, Ezzelino decided to have Cunizza back and sent a troubadour to arrange her escape. His choice was probably suggested by the fact that troubadours had free entrance everywhere and were beyond suspicion.

But this troubadour was an unusual one. Not only was he possessed of irresistible charm and exceptional good looks, but he was also nobly born, being the son of a Mantuan lord. Finding the aristocratic castle routine of the day tedious, he had taken to minstrelsy as a more entertaining way of life. His name was Sordello.

Enthusiastically seconded by Cunizza herself, the escape from Count Richard's court went off without a hitch, but the couple had fallen head over heels in love at first sight and so, instead of returning to Ezzelino's court, they went off together, causing one of the major scandals of the day.

The affair was passionate, but short-lived, for Count Richard had sworn revenge and Sordello was obliged to escape into Provence where he became the most sought-after of all the troubadours. When Charles d'Anjou came down into Italy to fight and defeat Manfred at the battle of Benevento, Sordello was in his train, and four years later Charles gave him the lordship of various lands in Abruzzo. So finally the nobleman-turned-troubadour reverted to his origins.

It is quite possible that Dante saw the now aged, but still passionate Cunizza about the streets of Florence.

Mass he attended with his family at the church of Saint John, and there he certainly heard much of Hell, for it was a common subject for speculation and exhortation. He probably knew of Saint Patrick's well in Ireland which was celebrated throughout Europe. Saint Patrick, it was said, had caused the well to be dug down to Hell at the centre of the earth to convince doubters. A very sceptical knight, the Cavalier Owen, had returned from a descent fully convinced and with the most appalling stories of the torments inflicted there. Dante would also have heard how Pope Gregory the Great had opined that Hell was reached through the craters of volcanoes and that Etna erupted lava to make room for more sinners.

Hell

Certainly no room was left for doubt concerning the reality and omnipresence of sin. In Santa Maria Novella a certain Brother Giordano announced that, out of ten thousand marriages, not a single bride or groom reached the altar with virginity intact. And unnatural vice was so rife that homosexuals were known in Germany as *Florenzen*.

But penalties for sexual crime were severe. Sodomites were castrated, and if their partners were minors they were also fined heavily and flogged. Those who pimped for male prostitutes had their right hand cut off and, for a second offence, their right foot. Informers were rewarded with half the fine, and torture was permitted to extract confessions. Parents who incited their sons to homosexuality had their houses burnt down. Yet for all their severity, these punishments seem to have had little effect.

Brothels were forbidden in the city centre and their inmates were not allowed to solicit there on pain of whipping and, for a second offence, branding on the right cheek. But in practice the whores plied their trade wherever they wished, provided that they avoided the religious houses and lepers. If they went with the latter they were burnt to death.

The boy Dante met Florentine violence young. A cousin of his father's had killed an adversary and then been slain himself in a vendetta killing. But for some reason at this point the usual chain reaction of vendetta killing halted. Possibly Dante's father was nervous for his own skin and no other eligible male was available. For years the family lived under a cloud of shame for this unrevenged murder.

Altogether Dante's future at this stage looked unpropitious. His mother was dead and his father was a small-time usurer. But fortunately there was food for day-dreams a little higher up in the branches of his family tree. His great-grandfather on his father's side had been a warrior knight, a martyr, a defender of the faith, 'in arms and wisdom most notable and valorous,' says Boccaccio. His name was Cacciaguida.

He had gone on the Second Crusade in the Holy Land with Emperor Conrad III and there, after having been knighted for valour, he died fighting against the Saracens. This was the background Dante needed. Beside it his father's shoddy dealings, the family's general mediocrity no longer mattered. Everything was suffused, transmuted in the dazzling light of his ancestor's glory.

Researching into his subject's boyhood, Boccaccio came across a story which was already famous in the city. It told of Dante's meeting with a girl who was to alter the entire shape of his existence. But all of eighty years had passed when Boccaccio began to write his biography, and the story was fast fading into legendary mist. Had the girl ever really existed? Everybody knew that Dante was much given to allegory, so perhaps this girl, too, was no more than an allegorical figure for love or theology. Boccaccio set out in search of the truth and discovered it just in time.

The girl was no allegory. She was a flesh and blood Florentine with name, family, home and an unspectacular and pathetic, but quite real, life story of her own.

The meeting occurred when Dante was nearly nine, and this is how Boccaccio described it.

'In that time when the sweetness of the heavens regales the earth once more with its adornments and makes all appear smiling with its many flowers mixed among the leafy green, there was a custom in our city that both men and women should meet in companies in their own districts to make merry. And so on the first day of May a certain Folco Portinari, a man much honoured in those days among the citizens, had gathered his neighbours together in his house to celebrate, and among them was the above-named Alighieri. And as small children are used to follow their fathers, particularly to places of merriment, so Dante, whose ninth year was not finished, had followed his. And together with the others of his age, for there were many in that place, both boys and girls, he gave himself up with his companions to childish amusements as well he might at such an age.

'Among that crowd of children there was a daughter of the above-named Folco, whose name was Bice (although he always called her by her full name, Beatrice) who was perhaps eight years old, most comely in her childish way, and in her bearing very gracious and pleasing, but with manners more grave and modest than are called for at such an age. Besides this her features were most delicate and admirably set in her face, and imbued not only with beauty, but with so much modest sweetness that she was esteemed by many to be almost an angel.

'She then— just as I described her, or perhaps with far greater beauty — appeared in this gathering, not I believe for the first time, but for the first time capable of arousing love, before the eyes of our Dante who, though still a child, received the glorious image of her with such love in his heart that from that day on, never while he lived did he depart from it.'

Dante himself also described the scene. 'She appeared to me dressed in a most noble colour,' he said, 'a rich and subdued red girded and adorned in a manner becoming to her very tender age.'

And at that moment the spirit of life in his heart trembled

and said, 'Behold a god stronger than I that is come to bear rule over me.'

As meetings go it was not all that spectacular, but it was to bring more fame to Florence than all her conquests, triumphs and splendours put together.

3

PAINT

The whole city glowed with colour. There were annunciations, nativities, crucifixions, ascensions, a myriad scenes from both Testaments within and without the churches, as though Christ and the Madonna, the apostles and prophets and kings were citizens of Florence, too, only brighter than the ones of flesh and blood.

Often they stood against backgrounds of gold which dazzled in the sun and set the Florentines contemplating the glories of Paradise or the splendours of earthly wealth according to temperament.

It needed a small army of craftsmen to make all these pictures, and although they were tough professionals who knew every rule and trick of their trade not many of them managed to make more than a bare living from it. The prizes for those near the top were tantalising, but few managed to climb that high.

One did. He climbed right to the dizzy pinnacle of his trade and — a yet more startling achievement — stayed there. He designed and painted the entire back-cloth and scenery for the Florentine tragi-comedy. He even built his own edifices to paint or sculpt upon.

This phenomenon was born at about the same time as Dante's meeting with Beatrice. Whether he was baptised Angelo, Biagio, Ambrogio or something altogether different nobody has the slightest idea, but he came to be known as Giotto, and under that name he was celebrated as the greatest painter of his age — of all time, some people said.

Boccaccio wrote of him that he had 'such an excellent genius that there is nothing given us by nature — mother of all things and operating power through the continual circling of the heavens — that he with pencil, brush and pallet-knife could not paint in a manner so similar to the original that it appeared not so much a resemblance, but rather the thing itself, so that many times in the work done by him man's faculty of sight mistook, taking that which was painted for reality.'

Giotto was born in 1276 in the Mugello valley about thirty miles north of Florence, though it might have been in another world from that of the furious Florentine snapping and snarling. His father was a peasant, shrewd, humorous and comfortably off.

A story tells how one day Giotto, while still a boy, had gone into the countryside about his home to look after his father's sheep, and while doing so had drawn a likeness of one of the animals on a rock. A man who happened to be passing saw the drawing and was so struck by the skill of it that he went straight to the father and asked if he might take the boy as an apprentice.

The man was Cimabue, the leading Florentine artist of his day; and so it was that the boy Giotto was brought to the richest and busiest workshop of the city.

Cimabue — literally ox-head — had enjoyed a fabulous career. As a boy he had been a compulsive scribbler, 'covering his paper and books with pictures showing people, horses, houses and various other things he conjured in his mind's eye'. He had played truant from school in order to watch some Greek painters who were working in Florence, and eventually had himself taken on as an apprentice by them. But they painted in the stiff, lifeless style of the period and he quickly outgrew them. And before long the Florentines, who were connoisseurs, were watching him with growing excitement.

The city had many workshops, but there was one *par excellence* — the church of Saint John. All the artistic forces of Tuscany had converged to make the mosaics of its dome, and this great creative sweep had reached its climax in about 1260 when the twenty-year-old Cimabue climbed up the massive scaffolding to work on the stories of Saint John the Baptist — the city's greatest painter (till a greater should come) at grips with its greatest saint.

From then on Cimabue's career had swept from triumph to

triumph, and he was called to many other cities to paint in churches and cathedrals. Soon the mere passing of one of his paintings was like a royal procession. Once when a Madonna of his was carried from the workshop to a church it aroused such enthusiasm that 'it was carried to the sound of trumpets and amid scenes of great rejoicing in solemn procession from Cimabue's house'.

On another occasion when old King Charles of Anjou was passing through he was taken, as the greatest honour the city could offer, to see Cimabue at work in some gardens. A large part of the population was allowed in with him and they jostled delightedly about the King to admire the work.

But for all his triumphs Cimabue was destined to be an artistic John the Baptist, falling with the rise of the shepherd boy from the Mugello valley. If Cimabue had known this, Giotto would probably have been left to scratch drawings on rocks for the rest of his life.

When Giotto came into Florence the city's great explosion of power, wealth and population was fully under way. The economic boom had created a colossal demand for labour which in turn gave rise to the biggest immigration wave in the history of the Italian communes. In the last years of the twelfth century the city's population had been 45,000; in the next forty years the figure doubled. Four years after Giotto's arrival the authorities decided to build a new city wall, the fifth since the foundation of Florence, but covering an area eight times greater than the preceding one of a century before.

Wool meant wealth. Florence imported the raw material from France, Flanders and England, processed it through all its stages and sold the finished product at a handsome profit. And as wool was the basis of all clothing in the Middle Ages this was big business indeed. As the money accumulated, it was lent out all over Europe at heavy interest, and so banking took its place beside wool as a massive twin column of wealth. Florence was the first capitalist state in Europe, and that was how they paid for the beauty.

One of the first things the money went on was building. As soon as he arrived, Giotto, who had a passion for architecture throughout his life, must have been enthralled by the tremendous amount of construction work going on. The whole city echoed to the banging of hammers, the sawing of wood, the chipping of stone. Little houses everywhere were being tumbled down to make way for vast and daring new projects. Wherever you went, masons and carpenters were swarming over the skeleton of some new church or palace. And every time a new construction was commissioned the builders received the same vital charge: 'Make it as beautiful as possible.'

That was what they were trying to do in Cimabue's workshop, even though Cimabue himself was not an easy man to work for. 'He had outstanding ability,' said Giorgio Vasari, the painter-author, 'but he was so arrogant and disdainful that if anyone remarked any fault or defect in his work, or if he noticed any himself . . . he immediately rejected it, no matter how precious it might be.'

This was the man whose word was to be law for Giotto over the next ten years, for the master of a workshop had the power of an absolute monarch over his apprentices. The paintings were meant to be a collaboration in which the master did the most important pieces. But some masters were lazy, and often in the contracts for frescoes and altar pieces it had to be stipulated just which pieces were to be done by the master personally (Giotto in his old age often did not put a single brush-stroke to his paintings).

The apprenticeship of an artist was like any other medieval apprenticeship and usually lasted a long time — if Giotto only stayed ten years with Cimabue, his own godson, Taddeo Gaddi, was later to work in Giotto's workshop for twenty-four years.

Giotto, then, started off as a general dogsbody, running errands, getting food and drink for his seniors, grinding the powder for the paints and generally learning the techniques and tricks of the trade. The first real painting job he did was to copy the works of established masters, mostly those of Cimabue himself.

By nature, Giotto was phlegmatic, with the patience and wiliness of his peasant ancestors, diplomatically cautious of giving offence to anyone who might be useful to him. And there is good reason to believe that these characteristics were already fully developed by the time he started to work for Cimabue.

He was famous, too, for his sense of humour, and one day

during his apprenticeship he harnessed this humour to his capacity for extraordinarily life-like reproduction by painting a fly on the picture they were working at. Cimabue tried to whisk it away several times before he realised the joke and, one may be certain, entirely failed to appreciate it.

There was no high-falutin' talk of art in Cimabue's workshop, or anyone else's either. The old joke about the frame being worth more than the picture was often literally true. Indeed, the frame was often commissioned first and the picture had to fit it.

Nor could artists be choosy about the work they took. They were quite used to finishing other people's pictures, doing religious and military standards, coats-of-arms and horses' caparisons. They would even turn out designs for ladies' embroidery.

For frescoes and paintings the contract was all important. It stated, among other things, the sum to be paid, terms of payment and date of delivery. Decisive in settling the price were the size of the painting and the number of figures in it. And the client would have to pay more if expensive colours like ultramarine and gold were used. The customer also chose the subject to be painted and usually laid down how it was to be done. The artist had few rights.

In this world Cimabue was the dazzling exception. Artists rarely managed to buy land or a house, and they almost invariably lived in poverty. Payments were small and, in the cases of monastic commissions, often made in kind — so much poultry for an Assumption. On top of this most painters had to live through long out-of-work periods.

Commissions for frescoed stories on church walls were common. 'By the grace of God,' said the artists of nearby Siena, 'it is our business to manifest to the unlearned the marvellous things worked in and by holy faith.' And in a sense the artists were more effectively propagators of the faith than the preachers. 'Paintings,' said the Dominican, Giordano da Rivalto, 'are the layman's books.' In fact, these frescoed churches were known as the Bible of the poor and every inch of wall space, even in the darkest corners, was given over to the telling of tales in glowing colours. It was almost by accident that some of the paintings happened to be of genius; many were just good craftsmanship; a few were not even that.

Formerly this story-telling in pictures had been done in mosaics. But now that the demand was so great that would have cost too much, so the friars relied exclusively on frescoes for which all you needed was plaster and colours which were cheap enough except for ultramarine — ground from lapis lazuli — and gold. Pig bristles were used for ordinary brushes, though for the more delicate sort you needed hairs from the innermost part of a squirrel's tail.

Nowadays most frescoes of the period are faded, while many are crumbling to pieces, but if you look well you can conjure up the vision of them as they were with their colours as brilliant as a field of wild flowers on a sunny morning, and actually see with your own eyes Christ bleeding to death on the cross, lying in the stable at Bethlehem, raising Lazarus from the dead. Or you can go further back than that and see the walls when they were still bare, and reconstruct the process of work as a fresco was painted.

Take a work done towards the end of Giotto's apprenticeship when he was at last able to work on the scaffolding beside Cimabue, as a collaborator. About them is a small army of apprentices and helpers, and the wall has already been covered with a solution of lime and sand mixed with water. On top of this Cimabue draws a series of vertical and horizontal lines in charcoal to divide the huge area of the wall into squares. He then goes on to make rough sketches of the basic elements of the composition, the principal characters, buildings and natural features. After this he sets to work with a reddish-brown pigment, doing a more detailed sketch of the entire fresco so that he himself and the commissioning friars may have an idea of the general shape of the finished product. The parts his assistants will do are more fully painted in than those selected for Cimabue himself.

Now the youngest apprentices have started mixing the colours and Cimabue organises the fresco like a military campaign. To one group of assistants he entrusts the sky, to another the earth and grass, trees to this one, a building to that, while for himself he keeps the principal human figures.

Now is the moment for a last thin coating of plaster which must remain damp until that part of the fresco which will cover it is finished so as to absorb and retain the colour. This coating is given every morning so that Cimabue has to make a precise calculation as to just how much work will be got through during the day. There should be no mistakes now, for this is the final version of the fresco.

First a dark, greenish-ochre base is painted, and over this the various shades, from the darkest to the lightest, until shapes and figures begin to glow in colour. Generally speaking, they work from the top downwards, starting with the sky, the tops of buildings and the heads of characters, moving down to ground and feet.

When they break off for short rests the friars bring in sharp-tasting wine with bread and cheese and a salame. The atmosphere, and often the language, are those of a building site.

4

FESTA

Before Giotto had started to scratch on rocks and while the thirteen-year-old Dante was walking about the stinking, rubble-strewn, though paved, streets of Florence, a papal emissary arrived in the city to try and make peace between the still warring factions there. He was a certain Cardinal Latino Frangipani, a renowned orator, a poet and musician to whom the composition of the *Dies Irae* has been attributed.

His first move, however, was hardly tactful. Having heard of the wild extravagance of dress and the orgies of self-display indulged in by the women there, he caused the passing of a sumptuary law designed to bridle this female extravagance and wantonness.

The Cardinal was a fool, the men must have reflected, if he thought that anything could induce thrift, prudence or modesty in women, particularly Florentine women.

In former times, it was true, the citizens of Florence were said to have 'dressed their women in the simplest of clothes', but if that had indeed been so once, it no longer was. One writer said that female neck-lines were cut down to below the armpits and added, 'All they have to do now is strip off their knickers and they'll have got rid of everything.'

Blonde hair was the rage, and the vast majority of women who were unfortunate enough to be dark spent hours in the sun trying to bleach their hair, but as a suntan was also anathema, they went to enormous lengths to cover the flesh, wearing, amongst other things, straw hats with broad rims and no tops. 'All day on the roofs,' they were reported as spending their time, 'some curling, some straightening, some bleaching — so much that often they die of catarrh'. The finished product was dusted with gold, reinforced with white and yellow silk plaits and put into nets decorated with flowers and pearls.

High foreheads were also fashionable, and those who were unlucky enough to have them low corrected nature's bungling with an ointment made from lime.

The dresses were outrageous indeed. One costume of the time was described as being of black and yellow material 'with birds, parrots, butterflies, red and white roses on it and many other figures of red and green, and with pavilions and dragons and yellow and black trees, lined with white stuff with black and crimson stripes.'

These dresses were cut in long, flowing lines which seemed to imitate those of the Gothic in the churches. Sleeves were very wide — 'sacks you might call them,' complained the same writer, continuing, 'When was there ever a more wretched, useless or detrimental style? They can't reach for anything on the table without filthying the sleeve itself and the table-cloth with the glasses they knock over on the way.'

Trains of dresses were of inordinate length, and as these, together with the Gothic line, required height while most of the Florentine women tended to be small, they remedied this with shoes that were little short of stilts.

The Cardinal set to remedying all this by ordering that neck-lines should be cut no lower than a few inches, that trains should be drastically reduced, that the hair should be innocent of ornament and that married women should go veiled. But no sooner is the law made than the way around it is discovered, as an Italian proverb says, and the Cardinal soon found that the women were wearing gauze-like veils woven with gold thread, far more expensive and seductive than their original head-dresses. And similarly all his other bans had been no less submissively flouted.

A diplomat by training, he ignored this defeat and turned to the relatively simple task of making peace. And in this he was to some extent successful, for things did seem to go better in Florence for a while. Trade boomed as never before. The guilds were gaining in strength, embodying the city's true personality. The great buildings continued to go up. And precariously peace flowered in the streets.

All this burgeoning prosperity and good will found their full expression in the celebrations for the feast day of Saint John, the city's still adored patron. These celebrations, on 24 June, were the greatest of all Florentine public holidays.

'In spring which gladdens the heart of the whole world,' wrote Villani, 'every Florentine begins to think how he will make glad the feast of Saint John.' The celebrations were not limited to the day itself, but could be considerably stretched before and after. Villani describes one such occasion in which more than a thousand people were involved day and night. 'They wore robes of white,' he says, 'and their master of the revels was known as Love. This company gave itself over entirely to games and pleasures and dances with ladies and knights and commoners, going through the town with trumpets and various other musical instruments in joy and merriment, feasting together both by day and by night. And this court lasted for two months and was the most noble and renowned ever held in the city of Florence, or the whole of Tuscany.'

Cimabue's apprentices, Giotto among them, will certainly have taken part in such events. They were prompt to festa all of them, and their doings, often outrageous, were an endless source of anecdote among the Florentines.

One of the apprentices was a certain Bonamico Buffalmacco, better known as a practical joker than as a painter, even though one writer did describe him as 'a very great master'. Only one work of his remains — a series of frescoes at Settimo and even they are almost entirely ruined, which might have pleased his bizarre sense of humour.

He must have been fairly good as a painter, for in one of the stories told about him a fellow artist called Bruno complained that his own figures lacked the life of Buffalmacco's. So Buffalmacco, to help him render his characters not only alive but actually talking, made him paint words coming out of their mouths. So began the custom of using words in pictures which makes Buffalmacco the father of the strip cartoon.

Like Giotto later on, Buffalmacco was often called to do special jobs out of Florence, and these sometimes gave rise to trouble. Once he went to paint a chapel in Arezzo and, leaving his work one evening, he returned the next day to find the painting unrecognisably smeared over. Twice this happened, and Buffalmacco put it down to jealousy, but when he hid to watch he discovered that the vandal was the bishop's pet ape.

For some reason this episode gave rise to a warm friendship between bishop and painter which was unhappily marred shortly after by a political difference. The bishop, a fierce Ghibelline, commissioned Buffalmacco to paint on the front of his palace the imperial eagle ripping the lion of the communes to pieces with its beak. But Buffalmacco, who was a no less fanatical Guelf, depicted the lion rending the eagle, and then escaped from Arezzo never to return.

On another occasion he went to Perugia to paint the city's patron, Ercolano, in the city square 'as magnificently as can be', as the contract put it. He had his scaffolding closed in with planks and matting — the custom of painters so as to protect themselves from the public stare while they were working — and started to paint. But after a few days the Perugians became so importunate in their efforts to see their patron saint that he lost his temper and gave the saint a crown of roach 'as big as ever came out of the lake'. He then skipped town, leaving behind another commune that would not be inviting Buffalmacco again.

Planks and matting were no protection against the curiosity of some nuns who peeped in to watch him at work and did not at all approve of his appearance. He was, apparently, 'as careless in his dress as in his life'. So, fearing that Buffalmacco was 'some tupenny ha'penny apprentice for grinding the colours', they got the abbess to tell him to send for the real *maestro*. Buffalmacco prepared a dignified-looking dummy with a paint brush in its hand and sat it up on the scaffolding. The nuns were delighted until 'one more daring than the others discovered the identity of this solemn-looking *maestro* who in fifteen days hadn't done a single stroke of work.'

At the same convent the wine brought him by a lay-sister was extremely acid. So he painted the faces of his characters pale and sallow, and when the nuns complained he said that in order to instil a bit more life he would need to mix the paint with the abbess's best wine, 'the best in Florence reserved for the sacrifice of the Mass'.

Contracts weren't always respected. One peasant, having

asked for and received a Madonna and Child, would pay with nothing more than promises. So Buffalmacco, using tempera paints mixed only with water, painted a baby bear over the infant Jesus. This had the desired effect, and then it was enough to wipe the painting over with a wet sponge for the baby to reappear.

Buffalmacco's end was a sad one. Old, destitute and ill, he was cared for in hospital by a company of mercy, 'and then when he died he was buried among the other destitute folk in the chapel of bones in 1340'.

Difficult as it was to scratch a livelihood from painting, some artists found it advisable to specialise. One had a profitable line in crucifixes 'especially those carved in relief, and what with finished ones and others in progress he always had some five or six at home, and he kept them, as painters do, on a table or long bench in his workshop leaning against the wall, one next to the other and each covered with a large towel or cloth'.

One day when this painter arrived home unexpectedly, his wife hid her lover on one of the crosses under the cloth. The husband, who had been warned of his wife's intrigue, ransacked the house from top to bottom in vain. Only the next morning when he went to his workshop did he notice two toes sticking out below the cloth. 'And looking among certain tools he used for carving he saw a little axe which just met his requirements. And taking this axe he drew near to the living crucifix to cut off the principal motive which had brought him to the house.' At this the crucified jumped from the cross and escaped with the cuckolded painter in hot pursuit.

Another married painter was Calandrino who figures in many stories. Calandrino was one of the world's eternal buffoons, always nose-led by fortune and his companions and always, at the same time, believing himself to be infinitely cunning.

Having received a small inheritance from an aunt of his, Boccaccio relates, Calandrino decided to buy some land with it. 'And he started dealing with the brokers in Florence as if he had 10,000 gold florins to spend, but of course it always fell through when they came to the price.'

Buffalmacco and that same Bruno who had lamented the lifelessness of his figures were colleagues of Calandrino's, and they suggested he would do much better to enjoy the money with them, but they didn't get so much as a meal out of him. So they teamed up with yet another painter, Nello, to get their revenge.

The next morning when Calandrino left home he was met by Nello who said, 'Have you been ill during the night? You don't look yourself at all.' Next he met Buffalmacco who told him he looked half dead, by which time he began to feel he was running a temperature. Then when Bruno came along, also insisting he looked dreadful, he was convinced.

Back home he went, and to bed. The doctor came — one called for him by his anxious friends — and after a brief examination said, 'Well, Calandrino, if I may speak as a friend, there's nothing wrong with you — you're just pregnant.' On hearing this, Calandrino screamed at his wife, 'You've done this to me, Tessa — always wanting to be on top! I warned you!'

'How shall I ever give birth to this child?' he wailed, 'Where will it come out? I should never have let her get on top!'

At last the doctor told him that there was a cure, but that it would cost something. Calandrino was willing to give everything he had, so the doctor demanded and got three pairs of capons in return for his medicine.

Another Calandrino story opens with a situation familiar to the journeymen-painters of the period. Bruno and Buffalmacco were painting at a rich man's country villa and, finding the work too much for the two of them, they took Nello and Calandrino into partnership.

The owner of the place had a son called Filippo who used the villa for taking girls to. One of these girls was a certain Niccolosa 'whom a sad fellow called Greedy-guts let out for hire'. One day when she was washing her hands at a well in the courtyard, Calandrino came out to fetch water and fell head-over-heels in love with her.

He confided his love to Bruno and asked if the girl were Filippo's wife, adding, 'I think she must be because when he calls her she goes into the bedroom. But I'd have a girl like that off Christ himself, let alone Filippo!' And so Bruno with Buffalmacco and Nello once again hatched a plot to fool Calandrino, this time taking Filippo and Niccolosa into the secret.

Later in the courtyard when Calandrino 'began to ogle Niccolosa and make such weird movements and gestures that a blind man would have realised the truth', she did everything in her power to inflame him further.

This went on for two months at the end of which, when their job was nearly finished, Calandrino realised that if he did not soon attain his end — as had been promised him — he never would.

'She's leading you by the nose,' Bruno told him. 'So if she won't do what she's promised, we'll make her whether she likes it or not.'

Calandrino was instructed to procure a sheet of paper, a live bat, three grains of incense and a candle that had been blessed. Having spent an entire evening catching his bat, Calandrino gave the ingredients to Bruno who drew some symbols on the paper saying, 'If you touch her with this writing she'll follow you immediately and do everything you want,' at the same time advising him to lead her into the barn.

Meanwhile Nello, who was a relation of Calandrino's wife, went off to warn her of her husband's projected adultery. 'By the cross of God!' she stormed. 'He won't get away with this!' And off they set for the villa.

When they were sighted, Filippo pretended to leave for Florence. Calandrino touched Niccolosa with the paper and she duly followed him into the barn. Once inside and with the door closed, 'she put her arms about Calandrino, threw him onto the ground and jumped astride him with her hands on his shoulders, holding him down.' At the same time she called out, 'Oh, my sweet Calandrino, heart of my body, my soul, my good, my rest, how long have I yearned to possess you and press you to my breast!'

At this Calandrino's wife erupted into the barn, Niccolosa escaped and the story ended among screams, scratchings and howlings.

Such was the atmosphere the painters of thirteenth–century Florence lived in.

It must have been altogether fascinating for a boy from the country like Giotto, and it is reasonable to assume that he was far too absorbed in it all to notice how, very shortly after his arrival, the Florentines were marshalling themselves for war.

He always was indifferent to the political scene.

5

WAR

On 2 June 1289 under a high blue Italian sky the most powerful armed force ever to leave Florence rode out of the gates to war. The trumpets squealed and the bells of all the city churches rang out in wild encouragement, chiming in with the bells of the war chariots. The red lilies on a white field of the city banners streamed overhead together with the white lilies of the French allies who rode with the Florentines, and the standards of five other Italian cities. There were 10,000 infantry troops and 1,600 cavalry, 'the best armed and mounted that ever went out of Florence'.

Ghibellinism had been destroyed for ever with Manfred's defeat and death at Benevento, but Ghibellines still existed, and the Florentines could not rest easily until they had been eliminated along with their cause. Siena, Pistoia and Volterra — all three formerly Ghibelline cities — had become Guelf, and Pisa — the ancient enemy of Florence and also Ghibelline — had been conquered by Genoa in a disastrous naval battle five years earlier.

So it was that practically the whole of Tuscany had turned or been won over to the Guelf cause. All except one city — the city of Arezzo whose citizens Dante was later to call 'snarling dogs, more fierce than formidable'. What now made them formidable, however, was the fact that all the Ghibelline forces remaining in Tuscany were concentrated behind their walls, building in strength and constituting an ever-growing threat to the other cities.

By now Florence was the traditional ring-leader of any concerted action in Tuscany, so it was she who declared war on Arezzo, but with her army rode contingents from Bologna, Pistoia, Prato, Volterra and Siena as well as the French allies.

The Florentines were briefly united against their common enemy, but their army contained all the leading human elements for the catastrophic civil war that was shortly to overtake the city.

A striking force of 150 picked men, on whom the first brunt of the fighting would fall, was commanded by a certain Vieri de' Cerchi. This Vieri was the head of a family which had been playing an increasingly dominant role in the affairs of Florence. They were *nouveaux riches*. About a century before a peasant ancestor had set up home in the city. Business was good, and by the beginning of the thirteenth century a grandson was already a senior member of the powerful wool-workers' guild. Then, by the next generation, they had a bank handling major deals with France and Flanders.

'Every member of the Cerchi family,' wrote the great Florentine historian Robert Davidsohn, 'did not fail on his death bed to repent bitterly of usury, ordering the restitution of what was, of course, only a part of the ill-gotten gains; and every generation continued to do business with the same lack of scruple which had characterised the previous ones.'

In the early part of its history the family had been barred from political office, so it had thrown all its ferocious energy into making money through trade, and when it had made enough, the political power came of itself. So that by the time Vieri rode out to battle, the family was already one of the most powerful in the city. It represented the aristocracy of money and hard work, and would have dominated Florence completely if it had not been for another clan whose blind and driving hatred it was the constant object of.

But although the Cerchi had come a long way from their peasant origins they still retained the rough ways of their ancestors, and the 'true' aristocracy of Florence regarded them with contempt. But they had the drive of their ancestors, too, and not long before the present events the whole of Florence had been gossiping furiously about Vieri's purchase of the noblest and richest palace in the city which he had then proceeded to wall in and enlarge.

The Cerchi had a wide network of relatives and friends, vast possessions in town and country, and they led a high life. The very government of Florence was housed in one of their palaces, and if they pretended no specific favours in return, it was no bad thing for the family fortunes to have the government in their debt.

Finally, for all their present power, their humble origins still won them the favour of the people. Dino Compagni, the chronicler, describes them as being gentle and courteous with the people, though he adds that they showed all the signs of too rapid a rise to power as well, being 'uncouth and ungrateful' with their equals.

Among the 150 men who rode under Vieri's command was a young poet named Dante Alighieri who was beginning to be known in the city for his songs.

A reserve striking force of 200 cavalry and a large number of infantry — which was to prove decisive in the battle — was commanded by another leading actor in the Florentine drama, Corso Donati. He was a descendant of that Aldrada Donati whose eagerness to marry her daughter to Buondelmonte had caused the murder at the foot of Mars and precipitated the calamitous dissension in the city. His was the family whose hatred and violence created a constant stumbling-block for the Cerchis.

Dino Compagni described Corso as 'A gentleman resembling the Roman Catiline, but crueller than he, of gentle blood and fine figure, a most delightful talker and exceedingly polite, of the finest genius, but with a soul always intent on evil doing.'

In fact, there were few of the numberless outrages perpetrated now almost daily in the city which did not bear his hallmark. Above all, he directed brilliantly executed forays of burning and looting against the Cerchi property. He had become so powerful that the people nicknamed him 'the Baron', and when he rode through the streets they all called out, 'Long live the Baron!'

As Dino Compagni put it, 'It seemed as though the whole city were his.'

Unlike the Cerchi, the Donati were of ancient and noble origin, and though they had been known to switch their political allegiance for expediency, they were feudal by tradition and character and deep-rooted belief. They had their family palace and political headquarters in the same part of the city where the Cerchi had established themselves in such style. Indeed, until the coming of the Cerchi, the Donati had been absolute lords of the manor, and there was no doubt that these *nouveaux riches* had put their aristocratic noses considerably out of joint. The two houses were practically on top of each other, and the Cerchi did their utmost to outmatch the Donati in splendour.

What with this and the political rivalry, hatred smouldered between the two families and any opportunity was good for fanning it. Corso Donati, on waking in the morning, was accustomed to ask, 'Has the ass brayed yet?' referring to Vieri de' Cerchi, and this and other similar pleasantries were bruited about the town. Naturally, they did not take long to reach the Cerchi household where they did nothing to pacify spirits.

Then there were Corso's burning and looting sorties which were swiftly reciprocated. The scuffles and clashes that broke out daily in the area gave it the name of the Quarter of Scandal. And when Corso or Vieri went by on horseback — they never walked — followed and surrounded by their escorts, the ordinary people, if they judged the moment inappropriate for obsequious cheering, ran for their houses and bolted the door behind them.

It was all very similar to another situation in another Italian city during the same period — the Capulet–Montague clash in Verona.

So Corso and Vieri had been at each other's throats for some while, and soon they were to be locked in mortal combat, but now, in a brief parenthesis, they were riding out together to fight on the same side.

Nine days after setting out from Florence, on the feast of Saint Barnabas — that same saint who had converted the city, which was considered to be an excellent omen — the Florentine force came upon the enemy. 'And the field of battle was on the plain at the foot of Poppi, in the district called Certamondo,' reported Compagni. 'And the plain is called Campaldino.'

The encounter must have been fairly unexpected, at least for the Bishop of Arezzo who, more at home on the field of battle than in his cathedral, rode with the army.

'What walls are those?' he is reported to have asked, being somewhat short-sighted.

'The enemies' shields,' he was told.

The commanders of Arezzo had chosen the site for the battle. Campaldino was the only plain thereabouts large enough for a full-scale clash, so in choosing it they made plain their intention of eliminating the other army. They knew that the enemy forces were greater than their own, but they took a calculated risk, over-confident in their contempt for the Florentines.

'They sought battle with them,' wrote another chronicler, 'not fearing for their greater numbers, but despising them, saying that they preened themselves and dressed their hair like women, and they held them in disgust.' Moreover, they had the cheering prospect that, if they did win, the Florentines and their allies, with only a solid wall of Alps behind them, would be cut to pieces.

Today it is possible to see an exact, three-dimensional portrait of one of the knights who rode into battle on the Florentine side and lost his life there. He was part of the French allied force and his name was Guillaume de Dufort. Realising that he might not return, he made his will before leaving. Among other things he left fifty florins to Amerigo de Narbonne who was commanding the entire allied force, and Amerigo was so touched by this that he had a sculptured marble tomb raised to his countryman. It is in the main cloister of the Santissima Annunziata in Florence, on your right as you go in under the porch. On it Guillaume de Dufort, his armour showered with the lilies of France, lies with his sword raised, eternally fixed in the instant before killing.

While they were mustering for battle, an officer on the Florentine side made a speech to his men which gives a good idea of the changes that were taking place in the art of war.

'Gentlemen,' he said, 'the winner in our Tuscan wars used to be the side that struck first and hardest. Battles did not last long and few men died because it was not the custom to kill. Now all that's changed, and the winner is the side which can hold out longest. So stand firm and let them attack.'

His assessment was accurate. The Arezzo force attacked, and their first charge was so violent that it seemed as though it were going to carry the day in one bloody sweep. It broke the battle up into a dense, milling series of hand-to-hand fights within the Florentine ranks.

Arrows rained down, and the air was so thick with dust that it was impossible to see further than a few feet. Moreover, it was unbearably stuffy. The sky was overcast and massive clouds lowered menacingly over the battle.

Somewhere in the thick of it was the song-writer, Dante. He was reported — by Leonardo Bruni, another early biographer — to have been 'fighting vigorously on horseback in the front line where he was in extreme danger', and in a letter written later Dante admitted that he was 'very frightened'.

This was hardly surprising. The new style of fighting, referred to by the officer in his pre-battle speech and introduced into Italy by the Germans, was a horror compared to the relatively chivalrous code that had prevailed before. The weapons were lances, pikes, iron clubs and huge double-edged swords. Death was infinitely to be preferred to the atrocious torments and slow haemorrhages of the wounded.

Having made the initial break through the Florentine line, the members of the Arezzo striking force now found themselves cut off from the rest of the army and hopelessly surrounded by the enemy. But they would not enter eternity alone. Taking out their daggers, they went on all fours under the bellies of the enemy horses, disembowelling them and killing the fallen riders, often at the same moment as they in return received the death blow. The agonised whinnying of the horses joined in ghastly harmony with the screams of the wounded.

The very success of the initial onslaught now worked against Arezzo. Before long its striking force was completely annihilated and the Florentines launched a counter-attack.

At this point two factors decided the day. Corso Donati, waiting with his reserve cavalry force, had been ordered not to attack, but characteristically he chose to disobey the order. He swooped on the flank of the Arezzo army, inflicting terrible damage.

This gave impetus to the Florentine counter-attack. But even now the army of Arezzo might have rallied and turned the day. There was a force ready to support them, the equivalent of Corso Donati's cavalry reserve. Its commander owned the castle of Poppi, the walls of which lowered over the battlefield. But this commander, seeing the havoc being wrought by Donati and his cavalry, gave the day up for lost and took refuge in his castle.

As Dino Compagni put it: 'Many that day who had been esteemed of great valour showed themselves to be cowards; and many who had never been spoken of won great esteem.'

This double blow was the end for Arezzo. Its army turned and fled, but was pursued and slaughtered in large numbers mainly, it is said, by the mercenary soldiers rather than the fellow Tuscans.

Nothing was left but the grisly aftermath. The plain of Campaldino was spread with the dead and the dying. Screaming and parched, the wounded lay in great pools of their own blood. When pain allowed them to think coherently, they were filled with dread of those wild beasts which infested fields of battle at nightfall when the conflict was over in search of defenceless prey.

Leonardo da Vinci noted much later the surprising frequency of great storms following these conflicts like celestial echoes of the human clash, so that the spectacle of nearby rivers literally running red with blood was not uncommon. One such storm broke now, and just at that moment the Arezzo commander, horribly wounded, staggered towards a stream on the field. He was called Buonconte da Montefeltro.

As he stumbled forward, his life blood spilled onto the battlefield from a gaping throat-wound. He did not get far, however, before toppling forward dead. The last word he spoke was 'Mary!'

Dante, inspired perhaps by a popular legend, describes what happens next. An angel and a devil, he said, swooped in together to gain possession of Buonconte's soul, and the angel succeeded in grasping it.

'Oh, you of Heaven!' shrieked the devil. 'Why do you rob me? You take the eternal part of him for a single little tear!'

And in the rage of his frustration the devil caused that same storm to break over the field of battle. The rain teemed down and, when the ground could soak up no more of it, ran in great rivulets into the stream. Buonconte's body was then swept by this stream into the 'royal river', the Arno, and buried in its bed under the mass of rubble and carrion washed away from the field of battle.

Along with Buonconte, all the other military chiefs of Arezzo — except for the excessively prudent reserve commander —

were killed at Campaldino, including the short-sighted bishop.

Another story tells how the priors of Florence were having an afternoon nap when they were awoken by a violent knocking at the doors, and a voice calling, 'Awake, for we have vanquished them!' But on rising they found nobody there.

They prepared a triumphant welcome for the home-coming army which arrived, to the sound of cheers and the wild pealing of bells, with 740 prisoners, the enemy's humiliated battle standards and the helmet and shield of the dead bishop which were solemnly hung as trophies in Saint John's.

And as the battle had been fought on the feast day of Saint Barnabas, the government decreed that a church should be built in his honour. Having converted the city, the saint now protected it in battle and so was deserving of honour.

6

LOVE

Between the triumph of Campaldino and the already looming tragedy that was to rend the city in two, there was a pause during which the Florentines enjoyed a riot of sheer living. A dangerously intoxicating feeling in the air seemed to suggest that Florence was the capital of the world. All that was most brilliant in Italy was now drawn to the turreted, medieval Florence with its sharply defined reddish-roofed buildings jumbled frenetically together against the soft green background of the surrounding hills.

Already there was something in the air of the prodigality and luxuriant delicacy of a new society. Courtiers and clowns poured into the city drawn by an irresistible attraction. Banquets went on uninterruptedly. 'No stranger passed through Florence, no person of fame or honour, who was not invited everywhere, with the citizens contending who should accompany him on horseback, within the walls or without as he wished or needed,' wrote Villani.

Travellers deliberately chose the Florentine route because of the hospitality they knew they would receive there, and later, back home, when they found Florentine products on the market, remembered hospitality made them buy the more readily.

Within this teeming commonweal there was a very small and closed circle of young men who were at the same time the golden lads of the city and its intellectual arbiters. They were all poets and, some time before Campaldino, Dante had been admitted to their exclusive company.

Their undisputed leader, the one on whose word alone

depended admission or exclusion, was an aristocrat named Guido Cavalcanti. His uniqueness was summed up by an anonymous writer who called him 'one of the eyes of Florence'.

He was indisputedly the greatest poet in the city at that time and he belonged to one of the oldest and richest families which had come to Italy with Charlemagne. The Cavalcantis possessed various castles outside the city as well as a large number of houses and palaces in the centre together with shops and warehouses which they rented out.

Many of the illustrious visitors to Florence were guests of the family, including the stupendous courtesan Cunizza da Romano. 'A very noble knight,' Villani described Guido, 'courteous and bold, but haughty and solitary and much intent on studies.'

It seemed, indeed, that Guido, having had all the good things of life bestowed on him at birth, was prevented from enjoying a single one of them because of a curse inflicted by a bad fairy. Boccaccio wrote of Guido's father that he was 'a rich and splendid knight who followed the opinion of Epicurus that the soul does not live after the body and that our supreme good is in fleshly delights'.

Something of this way of thought was inherited by Guido, and it tainted everything for him. He despised his social inferiors and loathed his equals and felt a singeing contempt for all forms of mediocrity. And he was obsessed by death. He was the first Italian poet to touch upon the affinity between death and love. He and his lady, in fact, were surprised by Love who had come from afar in the shape of a swift Syrian archer. First love drew sighs from her eyes to shoot into his heart. 'Then suddenly,' he said, 'Death appeared to me.'

Corso Donati the Black Baron, who had saved the day at Campaldino by disobeying orders, disliked Guido intensely and spoke of him contemptuously as 'the ramrod' for his stiff and haughty manner, and even went so far as to mount an unsuccessful assassination attempt against him. 'He feared him greatly,' said Villani, 'for he knew the greatness of his soul.'

This enigmatic voluptuary (for all his pride he shared a mistress in an open *ménage à trois*), this furious contemplative who was said to be capable of throwing stones at anyone who disagreed with him, this ultimately tragic figure was yet

another of those Florentines to be taken into consideration by
Boccaccio.

There was at the time, he relates, a drinking and whoring
group of young men in the city led by a certain Betto Brunelles-
chi. Betto was anxious to recruit Guido into his group, but
failed to do so, he believed, because of the stronger pull of
philosophical speculation. 'because he held much to the opinion
of the Epicureans,' said Boccaccio, 'the common people said
that his meditations were all directed to discovering, if he
could, that God did not exist.'

One evening Guido had walked down to St John's which was
then surrounded by a large number of tombs among which it
was his habit to meditate. There he was spotted by Betto and his
companions who made a mock cavalry charge on him.

'Guido,' they said to him, 'you refuse to be one of our
company, but even when you have discovered that God does
not exist, what will you have achieved?'

'Gentlemen,' replied Guido enigmatically, 'you are in your
own home and are therefore entitled to say whatever you wish to
me.'

He then vaulted over a tomb and disappeared, leaving them,
very understandably, baffled by his answer. But when they
complained that they did not know what he was talking about,
Betto, their leader, replied with uncharacteristic sagacity.

'It is you who don't know what you're talking about,' he said,
'if you haven't understood what he meant. Honestly, and in few
words, he has just hurled the worst insult in the world at us.
What do you see all about you? The tombs of the dead. This is
our home, he says, to demonstrate that we and the other
ignorant and unlettered men like us are, in comparison with
him and the other men of science, worse than dead men, and
therefore, being here, we are indeed in our home.'

There is an inconclusive note about the story which is frus-
trating but which nevertheless gives it an air of reality. If it had
been invented, it would surely have had a more satisfactory
ending; so something like that must have happened, and word
of it reached Boccaccio.

Dante first took his place in the charmed circle which rotated
about Guido Cavalcanti shortly after his return from the battle
of Campaldino. He wrote a sonnet and sent it 'to many people

who were famous poets at that time'. One of these was Guido, and his reply — a seal of almost royal approval — amounted to an invitation to join the Florentine Parnassus.

Dante's position as a young and celebrated poet then put him much in the position of a celebrated pop star today, for poetry was part of the city's life-stream. Lawyers, doctors, merchants, politicians, monks and nuns all wrote poetry. The Florentines thought in verse and even quarrelled and insulted each other in sonnet form.

Dante's verses were set to music as well and sung all over the city. 'Above all things in his youth,' says Boccaccio, 'he delighted in music and songs, and would most gladly frequent all the most excellent musicians of the time. And drawn by this delight he composed many pieces which these same people set to the most delightful and masterly music.'

This, together with the fact that he was a hero of Campaldino, made Dante a figure to be pointed at by women in the street, and any hint of a love affair in which he was involved was bound to arouse public speculation and comment. And just such an affair was shortly to monopolise the attention of the Florentine gossip-mongers.

Guido, Dante and the others of the circle wrote a style of poetry called the *dolce stil nuovo*, or sweet new style. Like that Provençal poetry from which it derives, the *dolce stil nuovo* deals with love. But whereas in the first the approach to the lady was one of undisguised sensuality, with the lady herself remaining modestly anonymous under a pseudonym (usually for the very good reason that it was her husband who paid the piper, or the poet), in the second the process was reversed. The lady's identity was no secret, but the love expressed for her was stripped of all sensuality; it was love of divine origin and a necessary part of all true nobility.

The lady Dante chose to write of was the now grown girl he had met on that May Day in Florence fifteen years before. And the tangled web which was woven about their relationship was about to become a source of endless fascination for the Florentines. For if Dante, Campaldino veteran and poet, had all the requisites for the hero of a great popular love story, Beatrice had them all for the heroine.

She was startlingly beautiful and belonged to the best Floren-

tine society, her father being Folco Portinari, a merchant, a
banker, a politician and the founder of the great hospital of
Santa Maria Nuova. She was also at the time married to a young
merchant called Simone de' Bardi, but this fact was completely
ignored by Dante and the watching public; husbands counted
for nothing in the lists of courtly love.

After their first childhood meeting, they had met again in
1283, six years before Campaldino when Dante was eighteen
and Beatrice seventeen. This second meeting, like the first,
took place in spring. 'Exactly nine years after the first appearance to me of this most glorious lady', Dante described it, 'I saw
her again dressed in shining white between two ladies who were
older than she. As they passed along the street she turned her
eyes in the direction where I was standing, all full of fear, and of
her ineffable courtesy, which is now rewarded in Paradise, she
greeted me, and such was the virtue of her greeting that I
seemed to know the utmost of all beatitude.'

It was in fact this second meeting which was the subject of the
poem sent by Dante to Guido Cavalcanti, and so it seems very
likely that Dante knowingly awakened public curiosity concerning the affairs of his heart.

But for all the gossip that went on about the relationship,
nobody for a moment suggested that it was not completely
pure. 'Most honest was this love,' Boccaccio wrote of it. 'No
libidinous appetite appeared in the lover or the beloved, either
by look or word or gesture.'

After the second meeting, however, the plot began to get
involved. The next time Dante saw Beatrice was in church, and
it happened that somewhere between the two of them was seated
'another gentle lady of very pleasing aspect'. Consequently as
Dante looked at Beatrice it appeared as though he were looking
at the other lady.

This did not go unnoticed. As he was leaving the church,
Dante heard someone say, 'See how that women torments him!'
And hearing the name of the gentle lady of pleasing aspect
mentioned, he hit upon the idea of using her as a 'screen' for the
public gaze so that his real love for Beatrice might remain
secret.

And indeed, he hid behind her for 'several years and months'
and, to make the whole thing more plausible, he wrote, 'several

trifles in rhyme for her.'

But eventually the screen love left Florence and Dante acquired another one; and it seems as though his relationship with her was altogether less idyllic for the whole thing became such a public scandal that Beatrice 'withdrew her greeting from him'.

But his love for her did not grow less. Shortly after this he was taken to a wedding party by a friend who thought to do him a great favour in taking him 'where so many women displayed their beauties'.

The episode is described by Dante himself. 'They were gathered there in the company of a gentlewoman who had been married that day,' he said, 'and it was the custom in Florence to keep such a one company when first she sat down to eat in the house of her bridegroom'.

'So,' continued Dante, 'thinking to please my friend, I decided to stay and wait on the ladies of the company.'

And then suddenly, without having seen her, he became aware of the presence of Beatrice. 'I felt a throbbing in the left side of my breast which spread throughout my body. Then, pretending nothing was wrong, I leaned against a fresco painted on the walls of that house and, fearing that the others might be aware of my trembling, I lifted my eyes and, looking at the women, saw the most gracious Beatrice.'

Some of the women present, realising what had happened, began to make fun of him, including Beatrice herself. And when his friend pulled him outside to safety, Dante said, 'I have walked in that part of life beyond which one cannot go with any hope of returning.'

With the passing of time this strange love underwent a slow transformation like a liquid in a hidden retort, and when the process was complete he described it to some ladies who asked him why he loved a woman whose presence made him suffer so much. Once, he replied, he had loved her for the joy of her salutation, but since she had withdrawn it from him his joy had come to lie in something which could not fail. 'In what?' they asked. 'In the words that praise my lady,' he said. In other words, the verse which Beatrice inspired had become its own reward.

Beatrice's father died in 1289 and Dante's grief, in sympathy with hers, was distilled into poetry. Then he fell ill himself and, struck by the thought that one day Beatrice must die, was taken by delirium and saw the haggard faces of women who said to him: 'You, too, must die!'

'And after these women there appeared to me other faces most horrible to see saying, "You are dead." And thus my imagination still wandering, I came I knew not where, and I saw wild-eyed women weeping in the streets, most horribly distressed, and I saw the sun grow dark and the stars turn to such a colour that it seemed as though they wept. And birds, flying through the air, fell dead, and the whole place shook with great earthquakes.'

And as he marvelled at this and feared, a friend came to see him in his dream and told him that Beatrice had died. 'And I seemed to go and see the body in which that most noble and blessed soul had been, and so strong was the illusion that it showed me the lady dead. And it seemed that women were covering her head with a white veil, and her face had an expression of such humility that it appeared as though she said, "I now behold the fountain-head of all peace." '

Dante then called upon death to take him as well, but instead he awoke from the vision and was comforted by the women who were in his room.

But reality was not far behind the dream. Just a few months later, at the age of twenty-four, Beatrice died in childbirth.

7

MARRIAGE

This strange love affair and its aftermath which led to a tormented marriage were conducted against a dangerous background. Trouble was brewing again in Florence, caused this time because, in the words of Dino Compagni, 'the nobles and the great ones of the city, swollen up with pride, wrought divers ills on the people, beating them and using other injuries.'

The authors of this persecution were the bankers and leading trade magnates, the new aristocracy of Florence which, like all new aristocracies, was often worse than the old. They took the law into their own hands and administered their own summary justice. One particular family, said Villani, 'in their own house in the Mercato Nuovo [the New Market] and the centre of the city, hung men up in ropes, and at midday put them to the torture.'

But the persecuted proletariat found an unexpected champion in a certain Giano della Bella, described as being 'of ancient and noble family, both rich and powerful'.

This Giano had a good background of political experience, but he was an idealist and he had an almost child-like faith in his fellow-men — two major drawbacks for anyone who was rash enough to dabble in Florentine politics.

It was said that he had good reason to dislike the new aristocracy, one of its members having tweaked his nose in public and threatened to cut it off for him. But whatever his motives, his actions were now unequivocal and succeeded in changing the entire political scene in Florence almost overnight.

He succeeded in pushing through legislation admitting to the city government the hitherto excluded members of the minor guilds, such as the innkeepers and the rag-and-bone men, the riff-raff of the city as the members of the upper guilds, like that of the wool workers, considered them.

This move won for Giano the adoration of the people — a dangerously two-edged sword as he was to find out — and the loathing of the upper classes who considered him a traitor.

After this, Giano had a new code of law drawn up designed to put an end to the tyranny of the rich. But as always happened in Florence, things went straight from one extreme to the other. The code was severe indeed. It banned the aristocracy from all government offices and decreed savage punishments (including confiscation of goods and demolition of home) for any members of the once dominant class who in any way ill-treated one of the people. And the testimony of two witnesses was enough to prove any accusation.

This was an open invitation to the proletariat to avenge itself on its former persecutors for all past wrongs, imagined as well as real. And the judges, mostly fawning and terrified of this newly unleashed power, were scrupulous in inflicting the severest possible punishments.

Giano's original and quite sincere intention — defence of the weak — had been laudable, but now things had got altogether out of hand. 'Your horse's tail flicks one of the people in the face,' the nobility complained, 'you knock against someone unintentionally in the crowd — is it right you should be ruined for ever for such trifles?'

All that was needed now was a demagogue to whip up the lowest emotions of the Florentine rabble. And one appeared. He was a butcher curiously nicknamed Sheep. 'A very big man,' Dino Compagni described him, 'bold and impudent, an endless talker who often made speeches in the city councils without being invited.' Under his guidance the butchers quickly came to outdo all the other trades in cruelty and corruption.

Meanwhile, however, the former great ones of the city, having had time to rally, were planning to put things to rights once more. They met together secretly, and at first resolved on the simplest and most classical solution. They would assassinate Giano. But then they changed their minds 'for fear of the people', said Dino Compagni. Giano was still too popular. So they decided to go about it more subtly.

Cunningly they drew his attention to the manifest injustices done by the butchers, and the idealistic Giano's reaction was predictably in character. 'May the city perish,' he is reported to have said, 'rather than that these things should continue!' And immediately he fostered laws against this abuse of power which, of course, lost him the support of the butchers.

Next they pointed out to him the improper conduct of the judges, and then that of other categories in the city. And each time, as he took the necessary action, they made sure that the people concerned felt they were being unjustly discriminated against by Giano. Quickly the tide of public opinion turned against him.

The affair reached a sudden climax when, as a result of blatant corruption, judgement was given for Corso Donati, the Black Baron, in an assault case in which he was plainly in the wrong. As Corso was the most vicious persecutor the city had ever known, this made the famous Florentine rage boil over.

Screaming death and fire, the citizens smashed their way into the seat of government, stole the horses there, broke into the offices and destroyed all the documents concerning criminal cases they could lay their hands on. They also howled for the blood of the totally innocent Lombard mayor and his wife, the latter being 'much esteemed and of great beauty'. The two of them fled over the roofs, only just escaping by the skin of their teeth.

Hearing of the riot, Giano, optimistic as ever, mounted his horse and rode off to quell it, relying on his popularity with the people, not realising how thoroughly it had been undermined. And in fact when he came to the scene of the riot those people of Florence whose champion he had been turned on him. He, too, only just got away in time.

The next day the entire city was against him. Friends advised him to escape while the going was good. Optimistic to the end, he left Florence, but waited some distance away from the city walls, confident that the misunderstanding would quickly be cleared up and that he would be recalled in triumph. Instead, the news reached him that he had been condemned to death.

Cured at last of his faith in the good will of the Florentines, he set off for France never to return.

Behind him in Florence he left the sinister butcher Sheep victorious, telling everybody how he had liberated the city from the tyrant Giano. 'Many nights,' Dino Compagni quotes him as saying, 'he had gone from house to house with a little lantern, co-ordinating the wills of men to form a plot against him.'

It was about this time that Dante began to be involved in the city's political life — an involvement which was to prove no less disastrous than Giano's which in many ways foreshadowed it.

Maybe he was invited to take part. One day, at the height of the Giano affair, he was visited by a deputation of city dignitaries. At the time, he says, he was thinking about Beatrice and 'drawing an angel on some board'.

'While I drew,' he said, 'I looked up and saw some men of considerable regard beside me. They were looking at what I was doing and, from what I heard later, they had been there for some while before I was aware of it. When I saw them I got up and, greeting them, I said, "Someone was in my mind just now and I was absorbed in thought." On this they departed and I went back to the angel I was drawing.'

If they had come to propose an entrance into politics, they cannot have been altogether unwelcome as he was eager for anything which would palliate his still acute grief. He had tried study, throwing himself into philosophy, theology, the classics and sciences — above all astronomy.

He read so avidly that his eyesight threatened to fail and he had to lie in total darkness for several days with constant applications of cold water. But apart from that his intensive reading does not seem to have told on him unduly, for Boccaccio says that 'though he studied without cease nobody would have supposed from his style and youthful company that he was studying at all.'

He had unusual powers of concentration. One day in Siena somebody gave him a book he had long been wanting to read and, there being nowhere else immediately handy, he settled down to read it on the counter outside the grocer's shop. There was a holiday in Siena that day and the noise all about him was deafening, with dancing and a variety of rowdy games, yet he read on from three in the afternoon till late evening, and when somebody asked him how he had been able to ignore the festivities he replied that he had not been aware of any.

Another story tells how, one day at Mass in Florence, he failed to kneel at the elevation of the host. Somebody immediately informed the Bishop — a characteristically Florentine act. Called to account for irreverence, Dante replied, 'In truth I was so absorbed at that moment in contemplation of what was happening on the altar that I have not the faintest memory of the motions which my body made or did not make.'

Study was not his only distraction. In May 1292 he spotted, or was spotted by, a lady at a window. Overcome with sad thoughts, he looked up to see if anyone had noticed his distress and saw 'a young and very beautiful lady looking at me from a window with such compassion, so it seemed from her appearance, that all pity appeared to be gathered up in her'.

And to himself he said, 'May it not be that most noble Love dwells with that lady?' There was, of course, remorse and internal conflict, but he concluded his monologue, 'This is a gracious, beautiful, young and wise lady, and perhaps Love has willed her to appear so that my life may find peace.'

Her name was Lisetta, and he allowed himself to be consoled by her until she pretended to take the place of Beatrice in his heart. And then, or more or less then, he got married.

'Who — ' demanded with baffled fury Boccaccio, the supreme misogynist — 'Who in the sweet air of Italy would escape from too great heat to cool himself in the boiling sands of Libya? . . . What doctor would try to abate a raging fever with fire, or cure a chill of the bones with ice or snow?' Yet these things, he said, were no more insane than trying to mitigate amorous tribulation with marriage.

In fact, however, Dante had been engaged to his future wife since the age of twelve. Such early betrothals were common. His friend, Guido Cavalcanti, had been engaged at the age of seven.

Dante's bride was a girl called Gemma of the Donati clan, a cousin of Corso, the Baron. Boccaccio disapproved of her violently, called her a suspicious, nagging vixen and said, 'Once he had left her, he would never again go where she was, nor would he suffer her to come where he was.' He also reported that Dante used to sit up till late at night studying, 'so that many times both his household and his wife were saddened thereby, until they grew accustomed to his ways and took no further notice'.

However, they managed to have four children — Jacopo, Pietro, Giovanni and Antonia. And another early biographer, Leonardo Bruni, who did not feel half so passionately about things as Boccaccio, says that Dante, 'having taken a wife and set to living a civil, upright and studious life, was much sought after by the republic'.

Bruni, who was no believer in warts, ignores the period of wild, almost pathological, dissipation which followed Dante's marriage. After Lisetta there were Violetta, and Fioretta, and a great many others, and with them he gave free rein to the concupiscence which, says Boccaccio, 'found most ample space in this admirable poet'.

With Beatrice's death the ideal which had sustained him since he was nine years old had been suddenly snatched away and, for a while at any rate, out of sight really did become out of mind. By his own account, he stumbled in the unaccustomed darkness further and further out of his way and deeper and deeper into a tangled forest of wretchedness.

His companion in vice was his wife's cousin, Forese Donati, nicknamed Bicci and brother to Corso. Between 1293 and 1296 these two rollicked among the flesh-pots (for Forese was an outrageous glutton) and in the stews.

Forese's father, Simone, was almost a legend in the city for a macabre fraud he had perpetrated. An uncle of his had died and he, fearing that he would be left out of the will, consulted a friend of his called Gianni Schicchi who was a noted mimic. Gianni advised postponing the annoucement of death. He then disguised himself as the uncle, popped into the dead man's bed and dictated a will in Simone's favour, at the same time bequeathing himself the best mare in the stables. That sort of thing was much in the family style.

Dante also came across a woman in the Donati household who made a considerable impression on him. She was Forese's sister Piccarda, whose tragic story had caused something of a stir in the city. As a young girl she had run away to be a nun in a convent just outside Florence. But her brother Corso had other plans for her. Taking an escort of hired cut-throats he broke into the convent (a sacrilege which meant damnation, but the Donatis took that in their stride), kidnapped Piccarda and dragged her home where he forced her to marry a peculiarly unpleasant political associate of his.

The relationship between Dante and Forese — part friendship and part animal snarling — was expressed in a series of poems, a poetic bickering, which passed between them. In the first, Dante refers to the chilly loneliness of Forese's wife in bed due, he implies, to her husband's impotence. Forese hits back with an allusion to the shady doings of Dante's father. Dante replies with a poem about Forese's debts which were leading him inevitably, he says, to prison or thieving. Backwards and forwards the insults fly. Forese accuses Dante of scrounging off everybody, including the Donatis, and Dante's answer to that one starts off: 'Bicci, son of I don't know who until your mother tells me . . .'

At a certain point Dante's conduct became so outrageous and the scandal he caused so public that he received a reproof (in sonnet form) from his best friend, Guido Cavalcanti. But at the point he had reached it is doubtful whether even this had much effect on him. What did pull him up with unpleasant abruptness was Forese's sudden death in July 1296.

At about this time, too, he collected together all the poems he had written about Beatrice and Lisetta and the nature of love in general, and strung them together with a prose commentary which is partly a treatise on the art of poetry and partly an autobiography covering his life from the age of nine to about thirty. From its opening line — 'In that part of the book of my memory before which little can be read, there is a section headed "Incipit vita nuova" ' — tradition drew the title of *Vita Nuova* ('New Life').

Exactly when he did this neither Boccaccio nor anybody else was able to discover. Nor could they imagine the thoughts that went through his head as he pieced together the story, and the dead ideal began to shine again through the black and choking mist of the intervening years. All he says is that he had a vision 'in which I saw things which made me decide to say no more of this blessed one until I could more worthily write of her'.

Then, he said, if God gave him life, he hoped 'to write of her what has never been written of any other woman'. Few people would ever have set themselves such an ambition. Only Dante could have achieved it.

8

JUBILEE

In 1300, when Dante was thirty-five years old and Giotto twenty-four, the influence of one man was to make itself markedly felt — though in very different ways — in the lives of all the characters upon the Florentine stage. This man was the most titanic figure on the international scene of his age. He loomed over the kings and princes and politicians of Europe, hurling excommunications about him like thunderbolts. He was Pope Boniface VIII and the Florentines looked upon him with understandable misgiving for one of his many ambitions was to swallow up their city for good and all in the heaving papal maw.

Everything this Pope did was on a vast scale, and when he conceived the idea of the first Jubilee Year of Christendom to be held in 1300 it was immediately destined to become the Greatest Spectacle on Earth. But in the steaming kitchens behind the scenes the fate of Florence was being worked out.

For his Jubilee, Boniface wanted only the biggest, the best and the most expensive, so when it came to finding an artist to paint a portrait of himself announcing the event he sent a representative to Tuscany to search out the superlative.

This man went about visiting all the most outstanding painters and collecting samples of their work. And eventually he came to the workshop which Giotto, now a master in his own right, had set up for himself. As he had done with the other painters, the papal messenger asked for a sample. Giotto took a piece of paper, dipped a brush in red paint and then described a flawless circle.

The courtier thought Giotto was making fun of him (or, worse still, of the Pope), but Giotto assured him that the circle would be more than enough. And it was. Boniface, as shrewd about painting as about politics, did not undervalue the capacity to execute a perfect circle without compasses, and Giotto was duly sent for. The story gave rise to the saying 'You're dafter than Giotto's O', the word _tondo_ in Tuscan meaning both circle and fool.

A lot had happened since Giotto's departure from Cimabue's workshop. While still working there he had met and fallen in love with a pleasant and sensible girl of the Florentine middle classes called Ciuta, and as soon as he became independent he married her.

The marriage must have been difficult at times when Giotto had to abandon his family, often for months on end, to go and execute commissions hundreds of miles away. But Ciuta seems to have put up with it well, and there is no evidence that Giotto, for all the chances that must have come his way, was ever unfaithful to her. He and Ciuta had eight children in all, four boys and four girls.

During the early years of his marriage Giotto was often in Assisi painting, among other things, the cycle of frescoes in the upper church dealing with the life of St Francis, and this made itself felt in the naming of his children. Two of the boys were called Francesco, which must have made life complicated at times, and one of the girls was called Chiara, or Clare.

By all accounts Giotto was, to use a simile drawn from his craft, no oil painting. 'Giotto,' Boccaccio put it bluntly, 'was ugly.' And it seems that the children took after him.

'Why,' Dante is said to have asked him one day, 'are your children so ugly when your frescoes are so beautiful?'

'My frescoes I make by day,' Giotto replied, 'and my children by night.'

Giotto cannot have had much time to paint in Florence before the call to Assisi came, though there was an Annunciation of that period in which he is said to have caught the fear and trembling of the Virgin before the Archangel so well 'that it appears she is longing to run away'.

Saint Francis of Assisi died in 1226, stretched upon the naked earth and covered only with a borrowed robe as a last homage to his lady poverty. Less than two years later, on 17 July 1228, the day after his canonisation, the foundation stone was laid of one of the richest basilicas in Christendom, built in his honour, thanks to the ferocious zeal of Brother Elia, the General of the Order.

Two years later the remains of the saint were taken there under armed guard, for neighbouring cities were itching to get their fingers on the precious relics, and laid in a small chapel in the centre of the transept. The Basilica, in fact, consists of two churches, the lower which contains the body, and the upper which was finished in 1253.

As soon as the building was up the friars started to have it frescoed. They called in all the leading artists of Italy. It was said that such was the devotion for Saint Francis that some of the painters offered their services for nothing. We can be quite certain Giotto was not one of their number.

Cimabue had already been there, with Giotto in his entourage, working in both upper and lower churches. Now it was Giotto's turn to be the master. Moreover, the first job entrusted to him was a continuation of the Biblical scenes started by Cimabue. The challenge must have been irresistible. First there was the more or less mute comparison which would be bound to be made between the styles of the old and the young master. And then Giotto, who always kept a steady peasant's eye to the main chance, could not have failed to calculate that the Franciscans, with their monasteries all over Italy, could become excellent customers if they were pleased with his work here at the heart of the Franciscan world.

The Biblical scenes took him five years on and off, with frequent returns to Florence. Then, when they were finished, the new General of the Franciscans made a new and startling proposal to Giotto. Would he paint the life of Saint Francis on the walls of the upper church? It was a colossal undertaking — to cover all the vast wall space with twenty-eight frescoes, all considerably larger than life-size, re-telling the most topical and best-loved story of the century for the armies of pilgrims who were already clamouring to see it.

Before Giotto set to work on these frescoes, the old tradition of painting, as exemplified by Cimabue, stood firm and apparently unassailable. When he had finished it, the revolution was complete. It was nothing less than an artistic *coup d'état*.

In a professional, business-like way, mustering and deploying his assistants with the shrewdness of his ancestors organising a rich harvest, Giotto created a world, and in that world for the first time the art of painting became entirely human. Later he was to soar to greater heights than this, achieve more mystical harmonies, but he would never again create just this atmosphere.

Francis dominates the cycle, but it is packed with lesser characters — lawyers, peasants, monks, prelates, girls and matrons. And, of course, animals, for it is a Franciscan story — donkeys, sheep, lambs, birds, and even a flying horse. The people express surprise and curiosity rather than awe, they sleep in a way that suggests snoring rather than mystical ecstasy, they sing full-throatedly, they chatter and, in one of the most famous scenes of all, a peasant throws himself down on a rocky mountain side to drink at a stream which Francis has miraculously made to appear for him.

The cycle is also indirectly a record of the life of the Middle Ages. The first fresco is a street scene in Assisi. The simple man kneels in the centre spreading out his cloak before the young Francis, but four citizens of Assisi who are watching curiously, perhaps a trifle cynically, put the whole scene squarely into everyday life.

Two little girls mingle with the crowd of baffled townspeople to watch the extraordinary spectacle of the naked Francis restoring his clothes to his father.

In another, Francis's prayers obtain for one of his friars the grace to rid Arezzo of the devils which have occupied it. The event is supernatural, but Arezzo is real enough with its citizens peeping out of the gates, the variously coloured, very solid houses and towers, the roof belvederes over which the bat-like demons flap away, even the swallow-tail V in the battlements which show that Arezzo is a Ghibelline city.

One Christmas at Greccio Saint Francis set up the first crib in the world, and a knight who was present at the scene saw the real infant Jesus in place of the doll which Francis had brought. Giotto sets the scene behind the altar of a church, creating an effect by showing the back of a crucifix which is hanging slightly forwards and facing the unseen western part of the church. It is a dazzling piece of perspective and the sort of trick which a young genius, giddy with his own power, would revel in. But the scene takes place in a real presbytery. The monks roar lustily, women peep timidly in from the main body of the church, some men follow the proceedings with curiosity, a lamb sniffs at the baby.

In the fresco showing the death of the knight of Celano, the table is fully laid for a meal such as it would have been in a well-to-do home of the thirteenth century on a white table-cloth embroidered with green stripes and hung with tassels.

For Giotto all this was a technical achievement to be satisfied with, a source of respectable earnings and a stepping stone to even more respectable ones. But he did not dream of considering it as more than a good job of work well done. When the call came from Rome, he left it without a qualm to be finished by his assistants.

The Rome that he now saw for the first time was a very different place from the Rome of today. Saint Peter's was a modest affair compared with the architectural colossus that Michelangelo was to build more than two hundred years later, and the space in front of it was of village-green proportions to the generations who have seen Bernini's square. The Lateran, the Cathedral of Rome, which had been destroyed and re-built many times, was soon to fall into complete abandon and then be damaged beyond recognition by fire. There was no Trevi Fountain, or indeed any of the great fountains of Rome. No Sistine Chapel, no stairway or church at Trinità dei Monti. None of the streets was paved, and the elegant Via del Corso of today was the scene of frenetic and usually lethal horse races.

Only the remains of imperial Rome stood out against the sky, stark, desolate and unappreciated, making Rome seem like a dead body buried in the ruins of its own greatness. It had a population of 35,000. No commerce or crafts flourished amid the miserable hovels in which the great majority of the people lived, and such productive activity as there was existed furtively in the city's undergrowth, hidden in the ruins of the ancient splendours.

What saved it from total misery was the Church. Ecclesiastics were continually buzzing backwards and forwards like bees in and out of a hive, and there was a steady stream of pilgrims who came to savour the honey.

So Giotto's first impression of Rome was not so much of the crumbling majesty of the past or even the squalid misery of the present, but rather the prosperous community of Saint Peter on the right of the Tiber between the Vatican and Gianicolo hills, a densely built area which stood out in sharp relief. At the centre of it stood the basilica built over the tomb of Peter which drew pilgrims from all over the world, and this coming year of 1300 was destined to draw more than had ever come since the saint had been nailed upside-down on his cross more than a thousand years before.

Here it was that the arch-enemy of Florence, Pope Boniface VIII, lived in unparalleled splendour, wearing robes sewn with precious stones and gambling frenetically with dice of pure gold. He was said to wallow in every sin from simony to sodomy and to be a professing atheist.

'Idiot! Idiot!' he is reported as having screamed at a priest who had invoked the name of Jesus. 'Jesus was a man like us! If he couldn't do anything for himself, what do you expect him to do for others?' Heaven and Hell, he affirmed, were on this earth. Hell was old age with its aches and pains and impotence. Heaven was youth and the enjoyment of young girls and boys.

But he believed in the devil all right, and hung himself all over with amulets and charms against the evil eye, including a ring taken from the dead body of the Emperor Frederick's son, Manfred.

His greed knew no limits, and he once violently upbraided a cook who had served him only six dishes on a day of fasting.

Above all he was avid for power. On his election he donned first of all the papal tiara and demanded allegiance as the representative of God on earth and then, brandishing a sword and wearing a golden crown, he claimed the homage due to an emperor. Nobody dared refuse it for, as one writer put it, 'He was loved by few, hated by many and feared by all.' The Umbrian mystic and poet, Jacopo da Todi, whom Boniface threw into prison, called him a latter-day Lucifer.

This was the man — a hale and stormy sixty-five at the time of his Jubilee — that Florence would now have to affront and Giotto to paint. And just as he was to do consistently throughout his long career, so now Giotto concerned himself with the business in hand and ignored politics. After all, he was a painter, and as a patron of the arts few popes had equalled Boniface in munificence. He had excellent taste and he expected that art should serve as a means of political propaganda for the church temporal. Giotto, who was accustomed to working to the rules of whoever footed the bill, would have seen nothing surprising in this. He always minded his own business and gave the customer what was expected of him (so long as the customer paid up, of course) and there is every reason to assume that he got on well enough with the Pope and never had to submit to any of the Pope's fits of uncontrollable rage — in one of which Boniface, offended that a mere friar had been sent in embassy to him, kicked the ambassador full in the nose.

Two million pilgrims came to Rome for the Jubilee, and 30,000 came and went daily. The small resident population saw itself increased by 200,000 overnight. Indeed, the scale of it was so enormous that the event is considered to be *the* festival *tout court* of the entire Middle Ages.

The whole of Europe poured over the Alps, re-grouped and provisioned itself in Florence or Siena and then rode, jogged, tramped, marched or dragged itself on to the capital. Many pilgrims made their wills before leaving, partly because of the length of the journey and partly because of the savage banditry which raged in the mountain passes. And many did in fact die or were killed on the journey. One centenarian peasant from Savoie had himself carried all the way by his sons.

'The husband went and the wife and the children,' wrote a chronicler, 'and they left their houses behind them bolted and barred, and all in a company out of perfect devotion they went to the said pardon.' For, whatever motives Boniface may have had in inaugurating his Jubilee, for the vast mass of Christendom it was a pardon. Whoever visited the tomb of the apostle for fifteen days (which did not have to be consecutive) received a blanket remission of all punishment due for his or her sins. (Residents of Rome had to make thirty visits.) The indulgence could be applied to the dead and was valid for those who died *en route*. The munificence of this was spectacular; hitherto indulgences had been partial, now for the first time in history (excepting only the total pardon granted to the crusaders) remission was complete for all classes and conditions of men.

The financial aspect of it was as overpowering as everything else. Apart from the undreamed-of wealth that poured into the purses of hotel keepers and private residents who stacked pilgrims into every available corner, there was also the money that was thrown into the coffers of the church. One observer reported seeing two priests before the altar of Saint Peter 'raking in infinite sums of money day and night'.

Rome was not built to hold such an enormous concourse of humanity, and in the early months a large number of people were crushed to death. Another gate was opened in the walls to relieve the pressure, but it appears to have done little good. Dante — one of the many Florentines who were there — was struck by the first officially recorded traffic-direction system in history. Pilgrims crossing the bridge at Castel Sant'Angelo were streamed to one side or the other according to whether they were going to or coming from Saint Peter's.

Not all the Florentines in Rome that year were there for the pardon. Corso Donati the Baron was there, looking up old contacts, making new ones, for it was here that his city's future was being decided. The Pope was surrounded by Florentines, for whom he had a weakness, calling them 'the salt of the earth'; however eager he was to capture the city, he had good reason to feel sympathy for the citizens. His bankers were Florentines who gave him vast loans at small interest. It was within these circles that Corso was planning the downfall of his native city and his own aggrandisement.

The final aim of all Boniface's manoeuvrings was the attainment of one vast and breathtakingly simple aim — a world theocracy with himself at its head. In the past the great opponents of this idea had been solely the emperors. But now a new force was thrusting itself between the Pope and the emperor and was daily growing in strength — the communes.

Everywhere these city states were gaining in independence and showing increased hostility towards the two supreme powers of the past. They were prepared to accept a helping hand from either one or the other as expediency suggested, but their final aim was to throw off the domination of both. And one city state stood out among the others — a Scarlet Pimpernel of liberty, more daring and more impertinent than them all — Florence.

The Florentines had even gone so far as to try, in their absence, three of their fellow citizens in Rome, *protégés* of the Pope, for high treason, and condemn them to enormous fines in default of which they were to have their tongues cut out. The sentence was clearly aimed at the Pope, even though no mention was made of him directly, and he knew it. On hearing of it he went into one of his violent passions of rage and unavailingly demanded that it be revoked.

If he could only crush Florentine liberty, he would have broken the ring-leader of the rebellion. He said explicitly in a letter that he intended 'to bring back the province of Tuscany to the law and ownership of the Church'.

And the man who could best help him to do this was Corso Donati. Corso, however, as he came and went among the dense, seething crowds of Jubilee pilgrims, was convinced that the Pope was helping the turbulent Donati clan he led. He did not realise he was merely using it.

9

SATAN

Jubilee year had not reached the half-way mark when the tragedy which had been preparing for so long in Florence finally unleashed itself. It was May Day, and everywhere the city was hung with flags. The girls wore garlands of flowers in their hair; in the streets and squares and along the banks of the Arno there was music and dancing. In courtyards little groups of Florentines were enjoying those endless, rowdy, jolly meals which have always been so much a part of Italian life, with plenty of cheering and clapping and singing, and the flasks of wine being promptly and frequently re-filled.

And into this delightful scene rode Satan in person.

That was the explanation for the sudden transformation from happy celebration to mob violence given by Dino Compagni, the little Florentine merchant whose modest chronicles of the city's doings lay hidden amid dusty archives for four centuries and then, being discovered, brought him sudden belated immortality.

'Because,' he said, 'it is easier to deceive the young than the old, the Devil, multiplier of all ills, joined a group of youths who were riding out together.' The youths with whom he rode were all part of the ferocious Donati faction, and when they happened to run into another group of young men belonging to the Cerchi clan the Devil's task was greatly facilitated.

From one minute to the next the revellers disappeared. Everywhere there was a slamming to of doors and the closing of bolts and chains.

One of the Cerchi had his nose cut off, only a few yards from where the young Buondelmonte had been killed at the foot of Mars. 'And that blow,' reflected Dino Compagni grimly, 'was the destruction of our city.'

The May Day clash flared into civil war — just the pretext Boniface wanted to send in a 'peacemaker' he had had up his sleeve for some two years, thus getting a papal foot inside the Florentine front door.

This was the moment chosen by fate for the election of Dante Alighieri to the office of prior of the city.

Love, poetry and learning by no means exhausted Dante's pulsing supply of energy, and ever since reaching maturity he had thrown himself into politics with the same passion that he dedicated to all his actions. As guild membership was indispensable for public office, he joined the guild of physicians and apothecaries, for which he qualified on the grounds that books were sold by apothecaries, and thereafter he had taken a regular but unsensational part in the government of Florence.

Just before the May Day clash he had been sent as ambassador to San Gemignano to persuade its government to send representatives for the election of a new captain of the Guelf alliance in Tuscany. A minute recording the adoption of his proposal still exists.

With these beginnings, there is every reason to suppose that Dante might have had a long and distinguished career in politics if he had not been elected prior in June 1300. At such a delicate point of the Florentine story he was not the ideal choice for high office. He was violent and intransigent to a degree, capable once, during a peaceful and scholarly discussion, of suggesting that somebody who disagreed with him should be 'answered with a dagger'.

During his research for the biography, Boccaccio managed to piece together a portrait of his subject. He was 'of middling stature and, when he had reached maturity, he went a little stooping, and his manner was grave and mild. He was always dressed in the plainest of clothes as became his age. His face was long, his nose aquiline, his eyes large rather than small. He had a heavy jaw and his lower lip jutted out. His colouring was dark, his hair and beard thick, black and curled, and his expression was always melancholy and thoughtful.'

As for food and drink, says Boccaccio, he was extremely

abstemious, 'both in eating and drinking at fixed hours and in never going beyond what was strictly necessary'. He delighted in solitude so that his thoughts might be uninterrupted, 'and if one that pleased him happened to strike him when he was in company, whatever might be asked of him he would not answer until his thought had been either resolved or rejected; and this occurred many times while he was at table or walking in company or elsewhere.'

But for all his seriousness and abstemiousness Dante was, so Boccaccio affirms, exceedingly lustful, 'and not only in his youth, but also in his mature years'. 'This vice,' he says, 'although it be natural, a common heritage and virtually indispensable, not only can one not in truth commend it, but one cannot worthily excuse it either. But among mortal men who will be the just judge to condemn it? Not I.'

Why did this solitary, abstemious, woman-loving dreamer dive headlong into the murky and sinister world of Florentine politics? The question worried Boccaccio. How, he asked himself, could a mature man, 'raised, suckled and instructed in the holy breast of philosophy, who had before his eyes the fall of kings, the desolation of kingdoms and cities, the violent whims of Fortune' — how could such a man not be proof against the vanity of human glory?

The answer is that Dante was ambitious. Politics had got into his blood stream and only total disaster could cure him. Besides, he had a passionate, overriding love of the city and he would have considered it contemptible baseness not to plunge into the thick of the battle where Florence was concerned.

It is typical of his destiny and nature that he should have been swept to the forefront at the precise psychological moment when prudence would have counselled keeping in the background.

No longer was the split in Florence between Guelfs and Ghibellines for the simple reason that there were no more Ghibellines. But the Florentines still could not live in peace together and so, just as in the original quarrel in Germany the lords had ranged themselves behind Guelf and Gibelin, the citizens of Florence rallied to Vieri de' Cerchi who had commanded the striking force at Campaldino or to Corso Donati who had led the decisive reserve cavalry.

The enmity between them and their families had continued undiminished and indeed was even fiercer after the brief period of collaboration imposed by Campaldino.

One incident gives a good idea of the explosive atmosphere which their quarrel was creating in Florence. A lady of the noble Frescobaldi family had died and the Florentines had gathered in front of the family home for the funeral ceremony. Benches had been set around the square for the mourners of gentle birth while mats were laid on the ground for the proletariat.

On the benches at one side of the square sat the Cerchi, on those at the other the Donati. The two clans eyed each other in silence. Then unexpectedly somebody rose from a bench, 'to hitch up his clothing', suggested Villani. But in that atmosphere even such an innocent movement was interpreted as a pre-arranged signal. Hands flew to swords on both sides and within seconds fighting had broken out all over the square with the people on the mats joining in.

The majority of uncommitted Florentines, believing the Donati to be the aggressors, gave their support to the Cerchi, offering to attack the Donati palaces. But Vieri de' Cerchi refused. It is said that he was always careful to avoid any victory which risked bringing political responsibility with it. If he destroyed the Donati with the help of a majority he might find himself forced into a ruling position, and Vieri had far too shrewd a knowledge of his fellow citizens to wish to rule over them.

This rejection of responsibility left Corso Donati free to do what he wanted and was thus responsible for the coming catastrophe and the downfall of Vieri himself.

In another incident of the period a group of young men belonging to the Cerchi clan died of poisoning after eating a black pudding. Nobody could prove anything, but it was generally held that Corso Donati was responsible, and tension and resentment continued to mount.

As the quarrel went forward the Donati increasingly took counsel with the Pope, while the Cerchi sought help and guidance from various noble families, thus laying themselves open to accusations of neo-Ghibellinism.

All the two factions now needed to formalise their promotion from gangs to political parties were labels. And two were conveniently at hand. Nearby Pistoia had recently been divided by a dispute within the city's dominant family whose members had emerged in open conflict and promptly been nicknamed Blacks and Whites. The same titles fitted the Florentine situation to a nicety, and so it was that the Donati and their followers became known as Blacks while the Cerchi and theirs were called Whites.

Willy-nilly, these two monopolised the Florentine political scene, so anyone wishing to have a voice in the city's affairs had to choose between them. Following his own nature, Dante would have rejected both and set up a third of his own. But this was impossible. As Boccaccio put it, 'seeing he could not maintain a third party which might in all justice lay low the injustice of the other two, bringing them back to unity', he joined the one which he believed had the most right on its side.

But how could he determine which one that was? He had strong links with both. His wife was a Donati, and his outrageous friendship with Forese had formed another link with the family. Besides, he had a natural pull to the political right which would have drawn him towards the Blacks.

On the other hand, his greatest friend, Guido Cavalcanti, was aligned with the Whites. Moreover, the Blacks were in favour of an alliance with the Pope (Corso had been soliciting papal intervention in Florentine affairs during the Jubilee), while the Whites — squalid, boorish, obtuse and money-minded though many of them were — were openly opposed to any concessions to the Pope.

This last factor was probably what turned the balance. Dante was a great hater, and he never hated anyone so unswervingly and whole-heartedly as he did Boniface. So by the time that the civil war broke out he was fully committed to the White side.

The Pope's first move when he heard of the Florentine clash was to send in one of his henchmen, Cardinal Acquasparta, former General of the Franciscans, whose task was officially to bring the two sides together in friendship. He was a friar by origin, though hardly in behaviour, and the Florentines could not hope for much impartiality from him. He was also said to be more fond of money than was becoming in a follower of Saint Francis.

Altogether he was not a man likely to appeal to Dante, which was unlucky as he came to Florence in the same month as Dante was elected prior.

Like Venice, Florence had woven an intricate cobweb of laws to prevent any single person from becoming too powerful. So it was that six priors were in power simultaneously, and they only held office for two months, during which time they slept in a dormitory and were not allowed to go home except in the case of a death in their immediate family.

But even so short a period as two months was more than ample for Dante to raise a storm of hatred about his head. He only realised this when it was too late. 'All my woes and misfortunes,' he wrote in a letter, 'had their cause and first principle in my period of office as prior.'

The already dangerous Florentine situation was exacerbated by two events which occurred about this time. The 23rd of June was the eve of the great Florentine feast of Saint John the Baptist when the city authorities and guild representatives used to go in procession to the Church of Saint John to offer candles. Among these authorities that year was the merchant-banker Dino Compagni who saw how a group of Blacks fell upon the head of the procession and beat up some of the civic dignitaries.

'We won the battle of Campaldino for you!' he quotes them as shouting. 'And in return you've stripped us of all the offices and honours in our own city!'

There was truth in this. Recent government policy had been consistently to keep the nobility for war (which they were good at) while limiting to the minimum their activity in the ordinary life of the city (where they were dangerous and overbearing).

Meanwhile Cardinal Acquasparta was going about his peace-making business. But his idea of peace seemed to be the exaltation of the Blacks at the expense of the Whites, and one day when he was sitting in a window at the Bishop's palace an arrow, shot from below, thudded into the frame a few inches from his head. He packed his bags and moved hot-foot to the more closely fortified house of a rich banker.

Most Florentines were only sorry that the arrow had missed. But the affair was a delicate one and Acquasparta, the pacifier, had to be pacified for fear that Boniface should be angered into overt hostilities for which they were not prepared. So the citizens, who always excelled in the art of scratching the right palm at the right moment, decided to offer him 2,000 florins in reparation.

The mission was entrusted to Dino Compagni. 'I took him the money in a silver cup,' he later described the episode, 'and I said, "Do not scorn it, sir, because it is small, for we cannot give more without full deliberation in council." And he replied that the offer touched him greatly. And long and longingly he looked at it. But he would not touch it.'

Then there was an attempted *coup d'état* organised by the Blacks in which one of the chief plotters was Simone Bardi, the widower of Beatrice. It was discovered and scotched in the nick of time, but had things continued like that the city would have torn itself to pieces, giving free entrance to the Pope.

Drastic measures had to be taken. An emergency government meeting was called, and it was decided to exile the leading members on both sides. While this meant getting rid of Corso Donati, for the moment at any rate, it also meant that Dante had to assent to the banishment of his greatest friend, Guido Cavalcanti.

In the marshes of Sarzana where he went, Guido caught malaria. His sentence was revoked because of the illness, and he returned to Florence, but only to die ten days later.

A few days before Guido's death, Dante's term of office came to an end. He stepped down seriously compromised and having made so many enemies that it formed a record even among Florentine politicians who had always accumulated enemies as effortlessly as a mangy dog picks up fleas.

At this point, said Boccaccio, Dante contemplated retiring into private life. It would have been better for him if he had, but 'he could in no way hold himself back from the sweetness of it, and so he continued to pursue the fleeting honours and vain pomps of public office'.

The internecine struggle was now reaching its climax and the city was already precipitating headlong towards the tragedy for which it seemed to have a febrile collective death-wish.

The Donati clique continued to intrigue at Rome and, with 'large sums of money mixed with false words', as Dino Compagni puts it, they persuaded the Pope to do what he had been wanting to do all along— to send in Charles de Valois, brother of the King of France, Philippe le Bel, as 'peacemaker' in Florence.

Valois had already gained a reputation for cruelty, ruthlessness and hard drinking. But far from uniting the Florentines, this threat of annihilation divided them even more and started them on a fatal course of shilly-shallying. They could have mustered many times the 500 cavalry which Valois was bringing with him. But instead they sent off embassies to him and the Pope.

Dante is said to have been part of the three-man embassy to the Pope. According to Boccaccio, when the job was offered, he made the characteristic reply, 'If I go, who will stay? And if I stay, who will go?'

The embassy was a failure. It could hardly have been anything else. Boniface had already unleashed Valois to achieve what he had been aiming at for at least four years, and he was not to be put off now by a mere embassy.

Meanwhile back in Florence the government seemed as helpless as a rabbit hypnotised by a snake. From nearby Siena, Valois sent an embassy to feel out the atmosphere in the person of 'a French clerk, a disloyal and evil man', as Dino Compagni describes him. And the Florentines behaved in such a lickspittle way that he 'realised that the faction that wanted Valois was greater and bolder than that which did not want him'. And he wrote to his master that the Blacks were up and the Whites were down.

The guilds were asked to vote on whether or not he should be allowed to enter the city. Slavishly they all said he should, 'except for the bakers, who said that he should be neither received nor honoured for he was coming to destroy the city'.

But the government ignored the bakers and sent to Valois, humbly inviting him to come and merely asking for his word that he would not install a dictatorship. He immediately gave it to them in a letter. 'And I,' says Dino Compagni, 'saw it and had it copied, and I kept it until his arrival, and when I asked him if he had written it of his own free will, he replied, "Yes, certainly." '

They even asked him if he would be so kind as not to come on All Saints' Day 'because on that day the people would be making holiday with the new wine, and disturbances might occur which, further stirred up by the ill will of certain evil-minded citizens, would upset the whole city'. The following Sunday would be more suitable, they suggested.

And even after all this cringing, the fame of Tuscan fury was still so impressed in his mind that Valois, the ruthless merce-nary who feared neither man nor devil, seemed to be still nervous of coming into Florence. He had to be dragged out of Siena 'almost by force'.

He arrived in Florence on Sunday, 4 November 1301, having thoughtfully allowed the people to finish their holiday of the new wine. He was riding on a horse with a silk caparison embroidered with the gold lilies of France, and he was received — to the blast of trumpets, the waving of flags and the throwing of flowers — by all the government of Florence who accom-panied him into the city carrying a gold canopy over his head.

And still he was nervous. Unable to believe that a city as powerful as Florence was meekly surrendering itself into his hands, he feared some plot and barred himself up with his followers in a house on the far side of the Arno where he would not be surrounded on all sides by dangerous, unpredictable Florentines, and he had the nearby bridge patrolled day and night to prevent a surprise attack.

His arrival was followed by a period of uneasy peace. Those who had expected instant slaughter were taken aback. Valois invited the priors to meals with him (they were terrified, but went) and even went to hear a friar preach about the patience and moderation of his saintly forebear, Louis IX. The pessimists said he was merely biding his time.

Then there came one of those signs in the heavens which held so much significance for the Florentines. 'At night,' says Dino Compagni who saw it, 'a most wonderful sign appeared in the sky — a brilliant red cross over the palace of the priors. Its appearance lasted for as long as a horse would take to run through two tournament fields. In this way the people who saw it, and I who saw it very clearly, could understand that God had turned against our troubled city.' It was Halley's comet.

In this atmosphere of ominous calm and superstitious dread just one false move was needed to unleash all the pent-up violence. It was made by a family whose name now appears in history for the first time. The Medici.

There was nothing noble about them in those days, even

though at their own level, which was a low one, they were beginning to make themselves felt. Hired by the Blacks, who were impatient to see the start of the bloodshed which would put power into their hands for good and all, they attacked a prominent White politician and left him for dead upon the ground. This enraged the people who clamoured for justice. But the authorities, afraid of the Blacks, refused to act. So the Whites decided to take matters into their own hands and barred themselves up in their houses and towers.

Now the city was an armed camp, and into it one November night there rode from exile the one man whose mere presence was enough to unleash conflict — Corso Donati, the Baron.

Accompanied by twelve henchmen he came and, finding the city gates shut, he broke in through — characteristically — a convent in the walls. Valois knew of his coming, but did not lift a finger to hinder him.

Corso did not even wait for dawn. He immediately attacked the houses of one of the rich families which had opposed him, running up his own flag on their towers. Then he broke open the prisons and enrolled their inmates among his marauding army. This was the beginning of six days' uninterrupted slaughter, looting and burning. It was during this orgy that the foundations were laid of the Medici family fortune, for they took a leading part in it, in one house stealing even the children's clothes.

In a pathetic attempt to restore order, the priors decreed that the great bell in their palace should be rung. Normally it served to call the people to arms, 'but it was to no avail and did not call forth the people who were greatly frightened'.

'Those who feared their adversaries took refuge in the houses of their friends,' reports Dino Compagni. 'Enemy insulted enemy. The houses began to burn. There was much robbing. Furniture and goods were hidden in the houses of people who, for lack of wealth, were less in the public gaze. The powerful Blacks extorted money from the Whites. Girls were raped. Men were killed.

'And when a house was burning fiercely, Master Charles [de Valois] would ask, "What fire is that?" and they answered him that it was only some poor hut when in reality it was a great palace. And this ill-doing lasted for six days, for thus long it had been established it should continue. And the countryside about burned on all sides.'

The pattern was that of all such violent overthrows. Many were falsely accused of conspiracy and were obliged to confess and hold themselves lucky to get away with a fine of a thousand florins.

'Many treasures were hidden in secret places,' said Compagni, 'many tongues changed their tunes in the course of a few days, many injuries were falsely spoken of the former priors by the very people who had before so highly commended them.

'Many became great through evil-doing who had before been known to nobody . . . neither blood ties nor friendship availed anything . . . nor were recent marriages any safeguard. Friends became enemies, brother abandoned brother and father son. All love, all humanity were quenched quite out. And he who shouted the loudest "Let the traitors die!" was himself the greatest of them.'

At the end of the six days a halt was called, more from satiety than from any desire to re-establish peace. A Black government was formed and set about legalising all the illegality which had been perpetrated and of course punishing all their political opponents from the previous regime.

Of all these opponents, the most outspoken had been Dante. But he had followed the dictates of his conscience. Consequently, the blow must have been stunningly cruel when, on his way back from Rome, the news reached him that he had been tried in his absence, found guilty of political corruption, inefficient administration, fraud and extortion, and condemned to a fine of 5,000 florins, two years' exile, interdiction for life from all public office and restitution of ill-gotten gains.

'In a single moment,' said Boccaccio, 'Dante was thrown down from the highest pinnacle of his city's government, and not only found himself brought to the ground, but harried thence.'

'This,' he cried with theatrical irony, 'was the marble statue they raised to the eternal memory of his virtues!'

Worse was to come. Dante didn't pay the fine because he could not and anyway would not. The time allowed for payment passed and he was left in default.

The next news that reached him from Florence was that he was to be burnt alive.

10

FRESCO

As far as Giotto was concerned Black and White were neither more nor less than two colours. Blandly ignoring the chaotic political scene in Florence he kissed Ciuta and the children goodbye and set off for Padua and what was to be yet another major triumph.

There was a family in Padua called Scrovegni. These Scrovegni were the richest and most powerful family in the city, and they had made their extraordinary rise from the humblest origins to the peak of the hierarchy entirely by means of usury.

The great architect of the family fortunes was a certain Rinaldo Scrovegni who had even been to prison for usury. But in spite of this he had managed to amass a vast fortune and raise the family to the apex of its power.

To keep his beloved money safe he had had a deadly booby-trap attached to the strong box so that a massive iron bar would smash the skull of anyone unwise enough to tamper with it. He died eventually, screaming in his delirium, 'My keys! My keys! I shan't give you my keys!' He was refused burial in consecrated ground.

His son Enrico then found himself with an embarrassing legacy. On the one hand there were the money and the position, which would have been acceptable enough in themselves. But on the other hand they were accompanied by the contempt and hatred of the whole of Padua. Rinaldo, like all true dynasty-builders, had been too thick-skinned and single-minded to care. But Enrico was of softer stuff. He minded when an outraged crowd stormed his house and set fire to it, even though the damage done in financial terms scarcely scratched the surface of the family fortune. He wilted beneath the displeasure of the Church. He decided to make reparation.

The commonest way to do this was to make some sort of votary offering. Another usurer had decreed in his will that a lamp should be placed before a crucifix painted by Giotto in Santa Maria Novella, Florence. But in this case it required more than a lamp to appease the Paduans and placate the icy disapproval of the Church.

Enrico decided to do things on a large scale. He would have a chapel built, dedicated to the Virgin, and on its walls he would have painted the entire story of the Redemption of mankind from before the birth of the Virgin to the Last Judgement. Only one person could handle such a colossal undertaking, and the fact that that person commanded an astronomical fee could not be helped. Giotto was sent for.

So, defending the cause of the great ones of the earth with his art, Giotto sealed a pact with them which was never to be broken for as long as he lived. His brush was at the service of high finance. And how else, he would have asked with ancestral shrewdness if anyone had put the point to him, how else could art flourish?

They say he not only painted the chapel, but built it as well — a theory borne out by the fact that it seems to have been specially designed for the great cycle of frescoes inside. Giotto's passion for architecture was already abundantly clear in his depiction of the life of Saint Francis, but this was probably the first time that he had been able to indulge it with real bricks and mortar.

In the Scrovegni chapel, Giotto's style flowered in its full maturity. The Assisi cycle, with all its zest and space, had been limited to the story of Francis and his miracles. Here he was dealing with the entire Odyssey, human and divine, of universal salvation. He and his workshop were entirely taken up with it for four years.

Giotto had practically unlimited energy, and he threw it all into this job. It is said that he completed the entire Visitation scene, dominated by five monumental female figures, in only six days.

As with the previous cycle, early fourteenth-century Italy

mingles inextricably with Biblical Palestine. The angel visits Saint Anne to announce the coming birth of the Virgin in the sort of bedroom that had been familiar to Giotto all his life, with its little bed, half hidden by a curtain, a low stool and the omnipresent solid wooden chest with all the household linen in it sprinkled with pepper to keep the moths out.

And as always in Giotto the lesser characters are as eloquent as the protagonists— Saint Anne's little maid sitting in the loggia outside, busily sewing, but looking sideways at the bedroom as though she were half aware that something unusual was afoot within, and the mysterious, tragic woman in black who is the fulcrum for the meeting of Saint Anne and her husband at the Golden Gate.

The Scrovegni cycle has one further claim to uniqueness. In it Giotto put on record for posterity the appearance of Halley's comet over Florence as it was described by Dino Compagni in 1301. In fact, in the Adoration of the Magi, the celestial pointer is depicted, not as the conventional many-pointed star, but as a glowing dull-red comet. If you examine it closely, you can see that Giotto applied the tempera and gold pigments in strokes which convey the appearance of the intensely bright coma (the nebulous envelope of the comet's head) and the thirty-million-kilometre-long tail as they were last seen by man in 1910 and will be seen again in 1986.

A legend tells of how one day, while Giotto was working at these frescoes, the Scrovegni porter came in and said that a man outside wanted to speak to him, and when the man was introduced, Giotto, all covered with paint, jumped down from the scaffold to embrace his exiled fellow-countryman, Dante Alighieri, who had just set out on his tormented wanderings from city to city.

This story seems highly improbable, however. Even if the two men ever met, their totally different attitudes towards the establishment would have seen to it that little love was lost between them.

Another story told of Giotto in this period describes a friend of his looking at a fresco of the Madonna and Saint Joseph and saying, 'Tell me, Giotto, why is Joseph always painted looking so sad?'

'Hasn't he every reason to look sad,' Giotto is said to have answered, 'when he sees his wife pregnant and doesn't know who by?'

Although this is far more in character than the Dante story, it is nevertheless startling. That such a remark came from the supreme painter of the gospel story may have had something to do with the stolid, down-to-earth attitude Giotto had inherited from his peasant ancestors. It may also have been that, working in Padua, he was affected by the climate of scepticism that prevailed in intellectual circles there. Averroism (the belief that the individual soul is only immortal insofar as it comes from and returns to a universal soul) had spread in the city, particularly among the doctors and at the university.

The Scrovegni series was one of the few that Giotto saw through to the end. When it was finished there was a ceremonial unveiling, and the huge crowd which had been waiting since dawn fell back in a stunned silence at the sight of such an unimaginable sweep of brilliantly coloured narrative. Then the silence was broken by an oceanic roar of applause, and Giotto was carried shoulder-high in triumph.

At the end of a solemn Mass, celebrated by the Bishop and attended by all the civic dignitaries, there was an enormous banquet, and the occasion was so memorable that it was celebrated in Padua every year for the next three centuries on 25 March. God had indeed written straight, somebody may have observed, with the crooked lines of Rinaldo Scrovegni's usury.

Shortly after Padua, Giotto achieved the greatest single *coup* of his life, winning a fee hitherto inconceivable in the world of painting to do a great mosaic of Saint Peter's in Rome showing the storm on the lake of Tiberias with Christ and Peter walking on the water and the fisherman's boat, symbol of the Church, nearby. As it was to occupy the central porch of Saint Peter's, it could be considered the central work of art of the whole of Christendom. Certainly Giotto's contemporaries believed it to be his masterpiece.

But the whole stupendous work crumbled away or was destroyed in the sixteenth century to make way for something greater in size if not in genius—Michelangelo's basilica of Saint Peter.

For May Day 1304, Giotto's colleague Buffalmacco, the practical joker, dreamed up the most spectacular practical joke of his career. He sent a proclamation throughout Florence announcing that anyone who wanted news of the other world should be present at a bridge on the Arno that evening.

The people came in dense, excited crowds. And there on the river, on a platform of boats, Buffalmacco had created a floating pageant of Hell.

'There were fires and other torments and martyrdoms, and men dressed up as devils, horrible to behold, and others who had the figures of naked souls, which appeared people, and these were put to divers torments, with great screaming and howling and storm, all of which was most odious and terrible to hear and to see.'

Then at the height of the spectacle the bridge gave way under the unaccustomed weight of such a great concourse of people, many of whom were thrown into the Arno and drowned.

'And so,' noted Giovanni Villani who chronicled the event, 'the hoax came true and, just as the proclamation had said, many indeed went in death to have news of the other world.'

This apocalyptic scene was a good expression of the general state of affairs in Florence. At the conclusion of the six-day orgy of murder and looting, led by Corso Donati and connived at by Charles de Valois, the Blacks established a regime of terror. Their courts passed death sentences with unheard-of rapidity — 560 in the first few weeks, made up of burnings, hangings and decapitations. Most of these were directly or indirectly the work of Corso Donati, now undisputed master of the city for all the nominal presence of Charles de Valois to whom he had presented trumped-up proofs of a White assassination plot.

The situation became so dangerous for anyone who was not a Donati man that even the powerful Vieri de' Cerchi had to flee together with the leading members of his party. But even in this emergency the Cerchi astuteness did not fail him, for he managed to put away a vast sum of money beyond the grasp of his fellow citizens.

With Cerchi and his followers gone, the Donati party enjoyed another orgy of destruction, ruthlessly and efficiently demolishing their homes.

The first major piece of news to reach the Florentines after the Valois–Donati *coup* was of the death of their greatest enemy,

Pope Boniface. It had not been a pleasant death, and the details of it must have caused a good deal of grim satisfaction in the city.

The indirect cause of it was a quarrel between Boniface and Philippe le Bel of France. Boniface had demanded temporal allegiance from Philippe. Philippe had not only denied it, but had the papal communication publicly burnt. Boniface hurled an excommunication at the French King. Philippe convoked a council which incriminated Boniface with blasphemy, simony, witchcraft, adultery and murder. He also organised a direct plot against the Pope.

On the night of 6 September 1303 a group of conspirators broke into Boniface's apartment, ordering him to appear before the council. His tremendous spirit unbroken, Boniface refused to yield an inch. 'Here is my neck!' he challenged them, 'Here is my head!'

One of the conspirators went so far as to slap the old man's face, and they then held him prisoner until a cardinal arrived with sufficient armed force to rescue him.

But the episode had broken him. He suffered atrocious pains from kidney-stones and it is said that his screams of agony could be heard all over Saint Peter's Square. But they were mixed with screams of rage when he heard the news that the Roman crowd had sacked the Lateran, removing even the hay from the horses' stalls. And so Boniface died, as he had lived, in fury.

The immediate result of Boniface's death, as far as the Florentines were concerned, was that they received yet another visit from a papal peacemaker, an honest one this time, Cardinal Niccolò da Prato, sent by the new Pope, Benedict XI. But all the Cardinal's honesty was not enough to bring peace to the Florentines, probably for the simple reason that they didn't want it.

The Blacks forged and distributed a letter purporting to come from the Cardinal inviting the now detested Whites and the phantomatic Ghibellines to invade Florence. The citizens rose up in fury, and the Cardinal was obliged to leave.

'As you wish to remain in war and malediction,' he is reported to have said in a parting shot, 'and do not wish to obey the envoy of God's vicar on earth, or to have peace and repose amongst yourselves, then stay with the curse of God and that of his Holy Church.' It was the sort of vituperation the Florentines were by now accustomed to.

The Cardinal had not been gone a week when there was a new outbreak of violence. Corso Donati, in spite of his apparent triumph, was still eaten up with jealousy and rage towards the wealthy families in Florence with pro-White tendencies. Above all the Cavalcanti family. But even he could do little in open combat against a family as powerful as that. So he decided to go about it in another way, by means of a sort of primitive fire-bomb made of sulphur and tar. A priest was chosen to launch the attack, a certain Neri Abati, a 'worldly and dissolute man'.

On 10 June this priest exploded his bomb in the middle of the Cavalcanti territory which was itself in the centre of Florence. The moment was well chosen. A strong north wind was blowing and rapidly the whole centre of the city became one uncontrollable blaze. It was said that more than one thousand seven hundred palaces, towers and castles were destroyed in the fire and 'the Cavalcantis that day lost their heart and their life-blood'.

Corso had achieved his aim. Not only had he ruined them, but he had broken their spirit. 'Saddened and much smarting', they withdrew to the houses of relatives, then abandoned Florence altogether.

But it was to be Corso's last triumph. Ageing now, tormented with gout and even more so with dreams of absolute power, he was ripe to fall. The Black–White conflict no longer had any meaning, for there were no Whites left. So the Black faction split, like a worm cut in two, with Corso and his clan on one side and practically everybody else on the other.

But this time the odds against Corso were too great. Besieged by the people, he raged furiously behind the massive walls of his palace. They worked an entire day to break their way in, and when they were about to do so the Baron escaped through a side door and rode out of Florence.

He was caught after a wild chase and brought back, but he refused to give up hope, 'defending himself with fine words' and offering his captors bribes in return for his freedom. But when they came near the city walls, realising that there was no hope for him, he suddenly spurred on his horse, at the same time letting himself slide out of the saddle. With one foot caught in a stirrup, he was dragged along the ground at a gallop. The torture was finally put an end to by one of the arresting party who rode up and drove a spear through his throat.

Left there for dead, he was taken in by the monks of a nearby abbey with just enough life in him, some said, to confess before dying. Certainly the monks sang his funeral rites. But few people were present at the interment of this man who had once been the be-all and the end-all for the city; 'for fear,' says Villani, 'of the authorities.'

So died, in a scene of violence that had been characteristic of his whole life, the evil but stupendous genius of the Florentine drama. With him as well as Boniface gone, it might have been expected that the Florentines could enjoy tranquillity at last. But less than a year later they were to face yet another major crisis.

11

EMPEROR

The news that a romantic and impractical princeling from Luxemburg was crossing the Alps threw not only the Florentines, but the whole of Italy into a state of violent agitation. Everybody rushed to take sides. The great lords of the north were for him. But many cities were against, and Florence was of course their ring-leader.

It was not that the princeling, whose name was Henry, was a particularly awe-inspiring figure. Nor was it even that his following — which included his wife, Margherite of Brabante — was all that imposing. It was simply that he had the title, though not yet the crown, of Holy Roman Emperor.

It was Clement V, a French Pope, who had been responsible for the election falling on Henry. Philippe le Bel of France, 'swollen with pride and believing that his power was feared by all', considered himself absolute master of Christendom, a delusion which must have been considerably fostered by the fact that he was holding the Pope and his court virtual prisoners at Avignon. If he could only obtain the crown of Charlemagne, the legendary crown of the Holy Roman Emperor for his brother, Charles de Valois (who less than a decade before had winked at the Donati rape of Florence) there would have been nothing to stop him.

So it was that, even though he was a Frenchman himself, Pope Clement felt obliged to stop this at all costs, and he did so by ensuring that the choice fell on the virtually unknown Henry of Luxemburg, 'forty years of age, of middling stature, a fine talker, well made but with a slight squint'.

To tell the truth, the title of Holy Roman Emperor was no longer worth much, but it still carried an almost mystical prestige, and it was this which made emotions run so high, particularly as his declared intention was to recall Italy to its 'rightful allegiance'.

The threat which Henry, invested with this mystical title, presented to their cherished independence was alarming indeed for the Florentines. True, he could do little with his own following, but if all the enemies of Florence ranged themselves behind him, then the situation would be desperate indeed. The city rushed to arms, mobilising immediately 10,000 foot soldiers and 5,000 cavalry.

She also set about financing all the other cities that were prepared to resist him. She sent, together with a large sum of money, a message to the people of Brescia that had a heroic ring to it. 'Be firm and constant in defending our liberty,' it said. 'Reflect on the ills that the German invader is planning for both our cities and remember the sort of people he has with him, hostile for centuries to you and to us by nature and by breeding . . . .'

The enthusiastic welcome Henry received on his arrival in Italy did nothing to reassure the Florentines. The Marquesses of Savoy and Monferrato went out to meet him. Cino da Pistoia quoted the Nunc Dimittis — 'Lord, now lettest thou thy servant depart in peace, according to thy word: for mine eyes have seen thy salvation . . . '

Dante, to the intense irritation of his fellow citizens, went even further. 'My spirit exulted in thee,' he wrote, 'and silently I said within me: Behold the Lamb of God, behold Him who takest away the sins of the world!'

Nothing could live up to that, certainly not Henry of Luxemburg, and in fact he quickly encountered his first set-back, the news of which must have caused a sudden lift of hope when it reached the city. He went first of all to Milan, where he was given a tumultuous welcome, for his coronation. But the crown of Charlemagne, which should have been in the Cathedral of Monza, had inexplicably vanished.

As an omen this was catastrophic, for the crown derived its mystical significance not from the splendour of its jewels, but from its very starkness, for it was a plain circlet of iron which was said to contain a nail from the cross of Christ.

Henry had to make do with a crown prepared by a goldsmith from Siena who worked day and night to get it ready in time. This crown was considerably more impressive to look at than the other, but it was not the same thing, and Henry, who was devout and idealistic, knew it.

(The real crown was found years later in the shop of an old Jewish pawnbroker to whom somebody in authority had pawned it, hoping it would not be missed.)

The inauspicious influence of the substitute crown was not slow in making itself felt. Henry was called on to arbitrate in a quarrel, and having given his judgement for one side, found all the supporters of the other side suddenly ranged against him. Milan, which had greeted him so unanimously a few days before, shifted uneasily beneath his feet, and drawings of the imperial eagle being hanged began to appear on the house fronts.

At the same time came the news that cities throughout the north were rising against him, their individual mutinies inspired, co-ordinated and largely financed by Florence.

The Florentines began to breathe more easily. And then they received a letter which aroused their collective wrath as it had never been aroused before by an individual. It was addressed to 'the most exceedingly vile Florentines within the walls' who had dared to defy their lawful emperor and thus, implicitly, God Himself.

If they continued in their wicked stubbornness, said the writer, they would only multiply the punishment that Henry would inflict on them. Their walls would be thrown down, their houses destroyed, their goods pillaged, their city laid waste.

Only one man could have written such a letter — the exiled White traitor, Dante Alighieri.

In the eight years that had passed since they had exiled him, the Florentines had heard various reports of Dante, none of them calculated to improve their exceedingly low opinion of him. He had almost immediately enrolled in a sort of Free Florence movement whose aim, however, was not so much to free the city as to overcome it.

At first this movement had undertaken a campaign of harassment. Severe drought had sent the price of wheat shooting up. So now White commando parties attacked the convoys carrying such grain as there was into Florence. The drivers were captured and the mules had their hooves cut off.

This sent the price of bread rocketing, but it also played into the hands of the Black government. It was not a popular government, and it would have been easy to raise sympathy for the exiled Whites. But now the Florentine man in the street learnt that the exorbitant cost of living was the responsibility of those same Whites. And any sproutings of sympathy he might have had instantly withered.

It will have given some satisfaction, therefore, to hear that Dante suffered from biting poverty. He was in lodgings with a fellow exile named Petraccolo whose little boy, having changed his name to the more euphonious Petrarch, was later to play a dominant role in the Florentine drama. As a man he recalled his boyhood meeting with the legendary poet-exile.

'He lived with my grandfather and my father,' he said, 'younger than the first, older than the second with whom he was hunted from his city on the same day and for the same political inclination. Often great friendships grow up between those who share the same tribulations, and so it happened with them, being drawn together, not only by misfortune, but also by affinity of talent and studies. The only difference was that my father resigned himself to exile, being absorbed with other worries and the problems of his family, while Dante opposed himself to it.'

In fact, after the abortive commando swoops on the grain convoys, the Free Florentine movement, with Dante still an active member of its organising committee, mounted a direct attack on the city itself. They raised an army of 6,000 infantry and 800 cavalry and launched it, first of all, against a castle only fifteen miles from the city walls which was taken by storm.

But the triumph was short-lived. As soon as an organised Black striking force fell on it, the Free Florentine army was shattered to pieces, the Whites threw away their arms and baggage in order to flee more quickly from the 15,000-strong force that was sweeping upon them.

Those who escaped were lucky. The others were taken to

Florence where the commoners had a comparatively merciful death on the gallows. But for the nobles was reserved that peculiarly sadistic revenge which the Florentines so delighted in wreaking on their fellow citizens. First they were dressed in rags and led through the city under a shower of insults and spittle. Then they were publicly tortured by the state executioner and his assistant and then at last dragged to the block, more dead than alive, for the final act.

Dante would have been burnt alive if they had caught him. Instead, as one of the leading promoters of the abortive assault, he was made scapegoat for the whole woeful shambles by his fellow exiles. It was even suggested that the Blacks had crossed his palm with silver florins to propose a delay in the attack in order that they might have time to build up their fighting strength. Dante was not the man to accept accusations of corruption meekly. He followed the only way his nature would allow him, abandoning that 'vain and malignant company' as he described them, determined henceforth to stand on his own.

It was as well for him that he did. A few months later, during a blazing July, the Free Florentines attempted another assault on the city, taking advantage of a temporary absence of the Black chiefs. Once again things started well enough. They came down discreetly from the hills and attempted to make contact with a White third column within the city. But the lack of co-ordination and the sheer muddle-headedness that had characterised the exiles from the beginning plunged the whole affair into catastrophe.

For some reason an attack was suddenly launched in broad daylight. If they had waited till nightfall when the third column would have been free to act within the city and the darkness would have brought a measure of relief from the pitiless July sun there might have been some sense to it. As it was, it was mass suicide.

The city walls were breached and the attacking force even got as far as the cathedral square. For a moment it must have almost seemed as though Florence had been 'liberated' at last. But then the illusion was shattered. The attackers suddenly panicked. The glorious delirium of the assault passed, and they realised that they were surrounded on all sides by Black forces. They attempted a break-through retreat, but many of them were hacked to pieces while others were taken prisoner and hanged. Some of those who did manage to escape are reported to have died of thirst in the arid wastes surrounding Florence.

The news of this latest fiasco, when it reached him, must have given Dante a certain grim satisfaction. By now he was staying at the Lunigiana castle of Moroello Malaspina, one of the Florentine commanders at Campaldino. Malaspina's hospitality was handed out irrespective of a guest's politics, which was just as well for Dante as the Malaspina strictly mercenary sword was currently at the service of the Florentine Blacks.

The castle life which Dante led here and with other families followed a regular, often spartan pattern. The day started at dawn when the lord of the castle rose and prepared himself — a simple process which took him less than three minutes flat. He did not wash — this was considered superfluous, usually immoral and, in the winter at least, extremely dangerous. As for dressing, he simply put on the shirt he had taken off the night before (there were no underpants which were only invented in the fifteenth century) and a robe on top of it.

The first meal of the day was served at about 10 a.m. in the largest room of the castle with the guests seated in order of importance. Children and old people were barred from these meals. The most important guests were served by the ladies of the castle who heaped their plates with pieces of wild boar, deer, goat, venison and other meats cooked in the huge ovens in the kitchen or on the spit in front of the fire, the whole thing highly spiced and washed down with massive quantities of wine.

The orgy was repeated at the second meal of the day in the evening and must have been a trial to the naturally abstemious Dante. This abstemiousness was responsible for a practical joke played on him while he was staying with the della Scala family in Verona around 1315. The head of that dynasty at the time was a certain Cangrande or Big Dog. On his orders a page hid at Dante's feet piling up all the bones which, as was the custom, people just dropped onto the ground when they had done gnawing them. When the tables were drawn back and this monstrous pile was discovered at Dante's feet, Big Dog said, 'I see this Dante is a hearty eater!'

'Sir,' Dante replied, 'you wouldn't even see the bones if I were a dog like you.'

After the first meal of the day, the lord and his party went hunting, and as they disappeared in the distance amid the clamour of horns and the beating of hooves, Dante probably returned with relief to study and write.

But the extreme licentiousness referred to by Boccaccio had not been dulled by age or exile, and he fell painfully in love on at least one occasion during the years of wandering. He wrote to Moroello Malaspina that the woman in question had robbed him of his sleep, his appetite and even of his free will. 'Why doesn't she howl for me, as I do for her, in the hot burrow of lust?' he cried in a poem. According to Boccaccio she had a goitre.

And on he went from place to place. 'Truly I have been a ship without sails and without helmsman,' he wrote about this time, 'blown to different ports, river-mouths and shores by the dry wind of sorrowful poverty.'

One day a friar called Brother Hilary, standing outside his lonely Camaldolese monastery on a mountain near Lerici, saw an unknown man staggering up towards the building. Brother Hilary asked him what he was looking for. At first he didn't reply. 'Then, after looking at me and my brethren who were about me, he answered "Peace."' That was how Brother Hilary himself described it in a letter read by Boccaccio who said the man was Dante.

Certainly the monastery was directly on the route that a traveller in those days would have followed going from Italy to France, which is where Dante is believed to have gone next.

'Seeing the way to a return [to Florence] closed to him on all sides and his great hope growing vainer day by day,' said Boccaccio, 'he abandoned not only Tuscany, but the whole of Italy and, passing the mountains which divide it from France, made his way as best he could to Paris where he gave himself up to the study of philosophy and theology.'

'Moreover,' adds Boccaccio, 'Dante was possessed of outstanding ability and an unshakeable memory, as he showed many times during debates in Paris and elsewhere.' It is said that he faced fourteen opponents all at once, debating fourteen different subjects drawn from the sciences and theology. He repeated each of the fourteen propositions in the order they had been put to him, answering or confuting each one exhaustively in turn. 'Which was held by the onlookers to be almost miraculous,' says Boccaccio.

He did not, however, get a degree. Boccaccio says this was because he would only accept one in his native Italy. It has also been said that he did not have the necessary money. He might well have stayed in Paris for the rest of his days if the news of Prince Henry's descent into Italy had not revived all his faded hopes.

To break the backbone of the resistance Henry should have attacked Florence. Instead, he unsuccessfully besieged Brescia, then moved on to Genoa where he received a triumphal welcome which cooled quickly when the Genoese realised that the imperial army had brought the plague with it (Henry's wife died of it) and that the Emperor was asking them for 60,000 florins to pay the expenses of his army.

Meanwhile Florentine provocation was passing all limits. Two imperial ambassadors had been denied access, assaulted and stripped of their horses and luggage. Henry was baffled by the situation. He had crossed the Alps with the intention of bringing peace and harmony, and now the whole of Italy was writhing tormentedly like a sackful of wild cats, and the wildest of them all was Florence.

He fixed a trial of the incorrigible city, inviting her to send two representatives to plead her case before his imperial throne. The invitation was ignored.

This was the last straw. He excommunicated Florence from his empire, declaring all Florentines 'children of Lucifer'. Dante was present when Henry issued this decree of excommunication, and he had also most vociferously thrown in his lot with the emperor. So the next Florentine move against him can have come as no great surprise.

The city had granted amnesties to thousands of the less virulent exiles in order to gain their support. She had also confirmed the sentences of the worst offenders. Among these was Dante.

Two killers were even sent after him, but his indentikit had been inefficiently prepared. Dante was staying at the time in a castle which rose near the Arno in the northernmost part of its valley. He had gone for a walk along the bank when the two assassins came upon him. Was that, they asked, the castle at which a certain Dante Alighieri was staying?

'It is,' he is said to have replied without turning a hair, 'and indeed he was there when I was last there myself.' And he went his way.

Finally, in September 1312, after two years of hesitancy, Henry did what he should have done at the beginning. He set siege to Florence. But by now the city was powerfully garrisoned, and Henry did not even have enough troops to cover more than half of the city walls, so that for the forty days it lasted the Florentines came and went practically as they pleased, taking in arms and provisions.

Henry's headquarters were at a monastery to the east of the city, and it was there that one day one of his commanders recalled an old prophecy concerning Henry which said that his conquests would take him to the world's end. 'The prophecy has already been fulfilled,' said one of the monks. 'This street is called World's End.'

As the autumn wore on it began to rain heavily. The Arno rose dangerously, hindering Henry's supplies and blocking the mills which made flour for his army.

On All Saints' Day he raised the siege. Florence had won.

Henry moved south to subdue Naples which promised to be an easier prey than Florence. But he never had the chance to try. In August of the following year, at Buonconvento near Siena, he suddenly ran a high temperature and died. Some said the cause was typhus or malaria. Others put it down to a poisoned communion wafer given him by his Dominican confessor who was, they said, in the pay of the Florentines.

12

MERCHANT

The situation was an embarrassing one. The merchant was quite willing to keep the child, but did not want the mother. The fact that the boy was a bastard did not worry him in the least. Many of the best people were bastards. Manfred, the Emperor Frederick's son, had been one, but that had not stopped him succeeding his father to the throne. One great lord had even christened his illegitimate child Bastardino, or Little Bastard.

But the mother was altogether a different matter. She was a widow by the name of Giovanna. Pretty enough. In fact, so pretty that before the baby had been conceived there had even been some talk of marriage. But now that was quite out of the question of course. She was altogether unsuitable.

At the time this child was born, Giotto had just finished his great mosaic of the storm on the Lake of Tiberias at St Peter's and was shortly to engage upon a new and yet more prolific outburst of creativity in Florence, while Dante continued his hopeless wanderings up and down Italy, also on the point of embarking on an enterprise that was to astonish the world. It was also the period of the unfortunate Henry of Luxemburg's ill-fated quarrel with Florence and his premature death.

The attention of the great majority of Florentines at this time, however, was taken up with none of these things. They were more interested in the weather. It had been so cold that the river Arno had been entirely frozen over and they had set up stalls on it, selling wine and salame and cheese. Fires burned on the ice, and the people organised all sorts of games and races.

But what with the ever-present challenge of commercial

enterprise and the particular problem of the superfluous widow, the merchant would have had no time for such frivolities which were hardly his style anyway.

He waited until the confinement was over and then informed her that her services would no longer be required, but that he would gladly undertake the boy's bringing up. Fortunately she quickly put an end to the awkward situation by dying — of grief, or so it was said.

That out of the way, the merchant was free to devote his entire time to trading and the raising of his son — christened Giovanni — as a suitable partner. To assist him in both he married an entirely suitable lady called Margherita Mardoli.

She was a member of the leading Florentine family of Portinari, which interested him considerably, and consequently a relation of Dante's dead Beatrice, a fact which, if he had known it at all, would have left him quite indifferent, for he abominated poetry.

It was to be of great interest, however, to his son who later on wrote the first biography of Dante and was able to call on the memories of his stepmother to establish the flesh-and-blood reality of Beatrice.

Boccaccio must have been aware of the circumstances of his coming into the world, but there was another version of his birth which he had invented himself and related in his writing and which eventually came to seem far more real than the truth to him. It was certainly far more interesting.

After all, his father often went to France on business, so why should he not have been conceived in Paris? And why should his mother, instead of being a mere superfluous widow, not have been a French lady of noble blood? Why not, come to that, of royal blood? And so, in Boccaccio's mind, it came to be.

Jeanette de la Roche, a tragic and beautiful scion of the French royal family, had given him birth. Fiction, as many bitter lessons in life taught him, was much more satisfactory than fact.

When Giovanni was seven, his stepmother had a child of her own, and it may have been the shock of this in an already unsettled childhood that made him take refuge in writing poetry. He had had the vocation, he claimed, *ex utero matris*.

'I remember that I was not yet seven years old, I had not yet read any tales or heard any teachers, I scarcely knew the alphabet when suddenly, through the secret workings of nature, I felt the desire to create, to imagine. Not yet knowing how a poem was made, I was already a poet.'

His father was appalled and redoubled his efforts to direct Giovanni's energies into something more profitable. And although the little boy was docile enough, the more he saw of his father's activities, the more he disliked them. Yet perhaps he owed more to his father than he ever dreamed.

The merchants were the pioneers of the Middle Ages, 'with open minds, swift intelligence and a solid base of culture, tenacious and bold in their aspirations which reared up in ambition and pride'. If the palaces and the cathedrals of the Middle Ages, the paintings and the frescoes, blaze out like beacons across the centuries, it was the merchants who provided the oil to make them burn.

They were the backbone of Florentine society. Their activities went on unhindered even during the worst crises, like the massacre under Charles de Valois. Indeed, it was their activities which had allowed the Florentines to survive and recuperate so that now there were a record two hundred establishments processing wool in the city as well as twenty banks. Florence's overall income was 400,000 florins and the expenses were 40,000. The population had mounted to 100,000 within the walls and 80,000 without. The city's prosperity flourished as it had never flourished before.

These merchants came from the people, indeed their origins were usually to be found among the dregs of Florentine society. They had no advantages of birth and, at the outset, every man's hand was against them. The aristocracy despised them and the Church looked askance at them, 'for never or rarely can a merchant be pleasing to God'.

There was also the vexed question of usury which was a mortal sin and included even the simplest forms of lending at interest. Aristotle, christianised by St Thomas Aquinas, had said, 'Money cannot produce money', and the third Lateran Council in 1179 had laid it down that 'usurers may not be admitted to the communion of the altar, and if they should die in this sin, they may not receive Christian burial'.

usury

The merchants, of course, found ways round it. The debtor, for example, agreed privately with his creditor to make restitution after the agreed period of loan had expired, thus making himself liable for a heavy fine which was not interest.

To make their way in a hostile world, the merchants had nothing to rely on but their own wits and courage. They struck out in all directions, wily, astute, intrepid, improvising as best they could in any situation that might arise, like the merchant going to Germany who was asked if he knew German and replied, 'No, but I can imagine what it's like.'

Their fortunes were usually based on some big, shady transaction or some downright criminal *coup*, as in the case of the Medici who had laid the foundations of their fortune during the six days and nights of looting after Valois had been called in. Maybe they would manage to buy up a huge stock of grain and then resell it at grossly inflated prices during a famine.

One typical beginning to a business career in the period was made by a certain Francesco Datini who left behind him 150,000 letters, 500 cash registers and various other documents.

Orphaned at the age of thirteen, Datini managed to scrape together 150 florins by selling his inheritance, and set off for the papal court at Avignon where he had been told that the streets were paved with gold. When he got there, he found that the land, torn by the Hundred Years War, was infested with marauding bandits.

With splendid impartiality, he started importing arms from Milan and Lyons and selling them to the forces of order and to the bandits. 'Fifty cuirasses for brigands,' he noted efficiently in one register. Before long he had opened four offices with a branch in Barcelona. His long and successful career was under way.

Travelling took up a great part of the merchants' time, and they daily faced innumerable and hair-raising dangers from flood and fire, shipwreck and avalanche. There were pirates at sea and highway robbers by land. The vast woods through which they had to pass were infested with wild beasts; packs of starving wolves prowled in the mountains which they had to climb. Plague often awaited them in towns, and malaria in the country.

Long trips abroad were full of imponderables. Merchants travelling to the east were advised to let their beards grow, take an interpreter and, if possible, have an attractive woman with them to pacify angry foreigners. When journeys were very long — it took nine months to get to China — it sometimes happened that the merchant died on the way which meant that the lord of the place requisitioned all his wares without compensation.

But the short journeys were quite bad enough. In the four-wheeled unsprung carriages which were generally used, it took more than two weeks to get from Florence to Avignon. Anyone who wanted to go faster travelled on horseback or, more frequently, by donkey which was the surest way in the mountains.

The roads were appalling, often no more than dusty or miry tracks, pitted with holes which made them a death-trap for the carriages. Hotels were rare and usually filthy, so the merchant either slept out or relied upon chance private hospitality or, most probably, in Europe at any rate, took the hospitality of the monks which was available on all main roads and mountain passes.

As if all this were not enough, the various authorities whose territory the merchants passed through imposed a bewildering amount of duties, taxes, tolls and often, because of the fierce rivalry that raged between the various cities, deliberately set out to make life difficult for any merchants who were passing through. Genoese consuls had to swear they would never knowingly transport foreign merchants or goods which might be in competition with those of their republic.

Transport could be prohibitively expensive. The price of a load of salt went up by sixty per cent in the fifty-mile journey from Florence to Pisa, and corn over the same trip increased fifty per cent. When there were rivers they were used and, as horses were too expensive, the barges were pulled by men.

But in spite of all this the merchants did make their way in the world, and the profits, when the various hardships, dangers and other obstacles had been overcome, could be colossal. The merchants who reached the top of their tree dominated the world. They were on equal terms with kings and popes, influencing their policies and their lives. One of the Valois princes said of the Lombard merchants that they brought with them 'not a ducat, but only a piece of paper in one hand and a pen in the other, and thus they shear the wool off the backs of the inhabitants'.

But the Florentines were, if anything, even wilier than the Lombards, so much so that Pope Boniface, whose economy was entirely based on their skill, had once described them as 'the fifth element of the world' (after air, water, fire and earth).

Like all men who have travelled on business since the beginning of human commerce, the merchants saw strange, wonderful or horrible things. They met with and observed a tumultuous, comical, passionate and ever-changing variety of sexual experiences, too. (The large crop of little girls in Florence with names like Piccarda, Francesca, Parisina, Borgognona and Tolesana indicated some of the various places where their papas had enjoyed adventures.)

About all these things they told stories, so that the whole of Europe was wrapped in a huge, invisible cobweb of anecdote. And Giovanni Boccaccio was caught in it from his earliest years.

13

USURER

Flea-ridden but majestic, the city lion had always attracted public attention and sympathy, and it is no wild flight of the imagination to presume that the young Giovanni Boccaccio, on the frequent trips the family must have made into the city from Certaldo, was among the audience around the cage

It was during this period that followed immediately on the death of the unhappy Emperor Henry that the Florentines acquired for their lion a mate who whelped two cubs, an event which, said the knowledgeable, was rare if not unique in captivity. As soon as they were born they went straight to suckle from their dam, and they immediately began to grow healthily and well. Everybody agreed that this was an excellent omen for the republic.

Another spectacle which drew enormous crowds at the time was that of Giotto painting his own portrait with the aid of mirrors, a stunt everyone held to be quite consonant with his sense of humour. Indeed, the whole city was buzzing with Giotto anecdotes, his *bons mots* being the more acceptable because they were so pre-eminently Florentine in character.

What did he see in the mirrors? In the Scrovegni frescoes there is a portrait of a man with a compact, well-shaped face, firm lips slightly parted in attention, light brown eyes looking upwards. This man is generally considered to be Giotto. The face is ordinary enough and not particularly ugly.

Yet contemporary accounts all agreed that Giotto was ugly. Boccaccio, later, even wrote an entire story based on Giotto's woeful appearance. Having pointed out that the most marvellous gifts of nature were often hidden beneath 'the most vile outward forms of men', he said how this very phenomenon could be observed particularly in two Florentines.

One was Master Forese da Rabatta, 'small and deformed in stature with a flat, squashed face', who nevertheless was so skilful in law that many eminent men held him to be 'a cupboardful of legal wisdom'. The other was Giotto. 'For all that his art was great, he was no whit the more comely in stature or appearance than Master Forese.'

Both men owned land in the Mugello valley (then considered to be the most beautiful stretch of Florentine countryside) where Giotto was born and Boccaccio set several stories. Having both gone one day to visit their property at the same time, they met and set out to ride back to Florence together.

It came on to rain and they took refuge in the house of a peasant. But as the rain gave no signs of stopping and they both wanted to get back to Florence that day, they borrowed two rough and ancient cloaks and two hats quite worn away with age. After they had gone some way and were soaked through and all spattered with mud from passing horses, the weather cleared up and they started to talk together.

'And Master Forese as he rode and listened to Giotto, who was a most diverting talker, began to observe him sideways and from head to foot, and seeing his appearance so wretched and downcast, without thinking about his own, began to laugh and said, "Giotto, if a stranger who had never seen you came along now, do you think that he would believe you are the best painter in the world, seeing you as you are now?" To which Giotto quickly replied, "I think, master, that he would if he could look at you and bring himself to believe that you knew the ABC." '

Many of the Giotto stories that were going the rounds had that unmistakable personal humour which had made him, as a boy, paint a fly on the picture Cimabue was working on.

In those days, on the first Sunday of each month the Florentines had a custom of going to the church of Saint Gallo, out in the country, not far from one of the city gates. The motive it was said, was not so much the indulgence which could be gained there on that day as the prospect of a country outing.

Giotto was on his way out of the city one first-Sunday morning when, having stopped in Watermelon Street to tell a joke, a herd of pigs from a nearby monastery passed by, and one of them suddenly dashed furiously between Giotto's legs, throwing him to the ground. Helped to his feet by friends, he turned to them unperturbed and said, 'Well, aren't they in the right? I've earned thousands of florins with their bristles in my paint-brushes and never given them so much as a bowl of soup.'

Giotto — 'the most sovereign master of painting of all his age', the man from whom 'limpid streams of painting flowed'— was now at the height of his fame and earning power. No artist had ever before commanded such fees. But this did not go to his head. The wiliness he had inherited from generations of peasant ancestors never relaxed its grip, and it created an extraordinary contradiction of character.

On the one hand Giotto was the supreme artist of the Middle Ages with whom painting soared up into the realms of mysticism. On the other, he was a ruthless usurer in the best Florentine tradition, if anything outdoing his peers in meanness, avidity and sheer outrageous rates of interest.

He bought houses and land and rented them out. He even bought looms and rented them to weavers too poor to buy their own, making an unheard-of 120 per cent profit when the highest normal profit from this activity in Florence was fifty per cent.

He stood surety for loans, and if the debtor was unable to pay, the creditor entrusted him with collection in exchange for which he took whatever property stood as guarantee. In 1314 he had six lawyers working for him in cases against insolvent debtors.

The sheer volume of painting (and travelling) he got through is even more surprising when one reflects that he seemed to spend most of his time in business transactions. In fact, painting and money-making were often of reciprocal assistance. For example, his dealings with looms put him in touch with a religious order which had a special interest in the wool trade, and as a result of this he did a number of paintings for their church.

Giotto the businessman was never absent from the workshop, where he signed all the paintings that were the exclusive work of his pupils. As a result of all this he was the only really rich painter of his age, and when his daughter Chiara married in

1326 he was able to give her a princely dowry of houses and land.

At the height of his creativity, he had a whole series of workshops throughout Italy, all producing simultaneously and many of the helpers in them, who often had to work quite independently of Giotto, had to be masters in their own right. Apart from the head workshop in Florence, there were other major ones in Milan, Rome, Assisi, Padua, Rimini and Naples.

Often Giotto had to leave one workshop for another while a series of frescoes was still incomplete, entrusting the finishing of the work to his pupils. Two hundred years later, Michelangelo had to do much the same thing, but for him this impossibility to be totally involved with his work right through to the end was a tragedy. Giotto, for all his fame, still belonged to the age of the great cathedral builders. For him a painting was a corporate production, though of course if one man's signature would help to put up the price, then by all means sign it, irrespective of who actually did the painting. In fact, the collaboration between masters and pupils of the period was so close that it is often impossible to tell who did what.

To make matters more complicated, Giotto often picked up local workers wherever he happened to be. These minor artists would come under his sway and then, when he had gone, perpetuate his style, adapted to suit their own bent and sur-roundings.

Whole families were absorbed into the great Giotto work-shops. One of Giotto's friends and contemporaries, for instance, was an artist called Gaddo Gaddi. This Gaddo had a son called Taddeo for whom Giotto stood as godfather. Then, when he was in his teens, Taddeo went as an apprentice to Giotto's Florentine workshop where he stayed for twenty-four years. And when he finally left, he was succeeded there by his son, Angelo Gaddi. The family affection for Giotto was so great that Taddeo used to sign his paintings with little bits of doggerel like: 'Taddeo painted here with colour and plaster, /Disciple he was of Giotto, the good master.'

Taddeo continued faithful long after the master's death when the style of painting at last began to change under the influence of Andrea dell'Orcagna. Yet another Florentine chronicler of the period, Franco Sacchetti, caught Taddeo as an old man talking shop with painter colleagues over a meal at the monastery where they were working. Orcagna himself put the question, 'Who was the greatest painter that's ever lived — Giotto excepted?' Old Taddeo's rather unsatisfactory reply — and one can see him gloomily shaking his head as he made it — was, 'This art of ours is getting poorer and poorer every day.'

If fame did not turn Giotto's head financially, it did tend to make him arrogant at times. Another story tells how 'a thick-headed workman' came to his workshop with a buckler saying he wanted his coat-of-arms painted on it. 'When d'you want it for?' asked Giotto and, on being told, said, 'Leave it to me.'

Contemptuous of a mere workman who asked for a coat-of-arms 'as though he belonged to the royal house of France', Giotto decided to give his customer more than he had bargained for. He sketched a rough outline on the shield and then tossed it to one of his assistants to paint. The finished product showed the humble accoutrements of a common infantryman.

When the owner returned and demanded his shield he was horrified. 'What's all this rubbish?' he asked. 'Rubbish you're going to have to pay for,' replied Giotto characteristically. The man refused and was unwise enough to take Giotto, the shrewd-est litigant in Florence, to law. Giotto counter-sued, wiped the floor with his opponent and got judgement in his favour.

This story shows Giotto looking down on a social inferior. But before him, painters did not have any social inferiors to look down on. He made himself and his art respectable. His patrons were the Holy See, the Franciscans, the communes and the rich merchant-banking families. He painted to suit them and was careful never to upset them and they, in return, acknowledged him and eventually, thanks as much to his business sense as his genius, accepted him as one of themselves.

Above all, he was careful to keep out of politics. It was meddling in affairs that should not have concerned him that had brought about Dante's downfall, and Giotto had no intention of letting the same thing happen to him. Anyway, politics did not interest him. But it says a lot for his powers of diplomacy that, in a situation where Florence and the Holy See were mortal enemies, Giotto managed to retain the good graces of both.

Before him, painters were considered too inferior to belong to one of the guilds. But in 1327 he was enrolled in the guild of physicians and apothecaries (the same guild as Dante had enrolled in), presumably on the grounds that a painter, having to grind his colours with pestles and mortar and have a certain elementary knowledge of minerals and mixtures, could be suitably classified with the apothecaries. This promotion in the social scale allowed painters to take an active part in public life. Giotto was careful not to take advantage of his new privilege.

It was also during the period of Giovanni Boccaccio's early boyhood visits to Florence from Certaldo that Giotto interrupted his travels for a while to execute two major new commissions in the city.

The two richest Florentine families were now the Bardis (for whom Boccaccio's father had started working) and the Peruzzis. Both were bankers. They held the financial strings of all the courts in Europe, including the English, and they had the monopoly of papal banking affairs.

It was these two families which now commissioned Giotto simultaneously to paint their private chapels in Santa Croce, the most resplendent of all Franciscan churches and a sort of Florentine Westminster Abbey. The Peruzzis asked him to do the stories of Saint John the Baptist and Saint John the Evangelist. The Bardis asked for Saint Francis.

So, after a quarter of a century, Giotto was back with the subject which had given his career such a spectacular lift-off. But between the two cycles there yawns an abyss. The first is a magic world of breathtaking miracles and sweeping uncommonsensical brilliance in which bat-like devils swarm into the sky, fiery characters ride through the air, a doll comes to life, Francis strips naked in the centre of the city, challenges the Sultan's magicians to walk into the fire with him and preaches to the birds.

The second is Saint Francis of the Establishment who would never dream of talking with birds (what sort of an overdraft would you give to a man who did things like that?) but consorts rather with the mighty ones of the earth. This was now the world that Giotto was on familiar terms with and that recognised him as one of its own.

Scarcely were the Bardi and Peruzzi commissions finished than another dazzling invitation dropped at his feet. Robert of Anjou, King of Naples, wanted him at all costs to decorate the convent and royal church of Saint Clare in Naples.

By now Giotto had received so many brilliant invitations, and the years were beginning to weigh on his shoulders so that he must have felt the temptation to stay at home this time. He was surrounded by a large, contented bourgeois family. Ciuta was resignedly growing old beside him. His eldest daughter, Caterina, had married a painter. Lucia and Chiara had gone back to the family roots, marrying wealthy land-owners in the Mugello valley. The fourth girl, Bice, who was a Franciscan tertiary, stayed at home helping her mother. Two of the boys had gone back to their grandfather's work on the land. The elder of the two Francescos helped in the administration of his father's affairs while the younger had taken up painting.

It would have been pleasant to stay with them, but Giotto was tough and had by now formed a life-long habit of answering the calls of rich patrons. He packed up yet again and set off for Naples.

14

HELL

Some time during his boyhood, Giovanni Boccaccio heard for the first time snatches of a strange and terrifying story which was to be perhaps the greatest single influence in his life. The writer of this story told how, while still in the body, he went down through Hell, circle by circle, to its icy depths where the eternal beating of Lucifer's giant bat-like wings keeps the Lake of Cocytus forever frozen.

Indeed, not only Boccaccio, but all the Florentines found the story a great deal more than a mere literary sensation. For one thing, few people doubted that the journey had actually taken place, that real torments had really been witnessed. For another, there was the identity of the author who was none other than that nigger in the Florentine wood-pile, Dante Alighieri.

By now his fame was beginning to spread throughout Italy. Some women in Verona are said to have pointed him out in the streets, whispering that his swarthiness was a direct result of exposure to the fires which burnt in the upper regions of Hell. But naturally the sensation was particularly felt in Florence — if for no other reason because Dante had reported the presence in Hell of such a large number of people whose names were household words in the city.

Ciacco, the now legendary Florentine glutton, was there, wallowing in the mud, lashed by perpetual rain and mauled by the three-headed dog, Cerberus. And in the burning tombs reserved for the heretics, Dante had seen one of the city's greatest Ghibelline leaders — a sort of Florentine Churchill — together with Cavalcante dei Cavalcanti, Guido's father and famous for his Epicureanism. Gianni Schicchi, who had dressed up as a dead man in order to falsify a will, had been seen hunting rabidly in the trench of the falsifiers.

All these stories, circulating first by word of mouth, created outrage, delight or amusement according to the audience, but always absorbed interest.

Then copies of the opening cantos filtered into Florence and people began to hear the actual words with which the story was told. Two things immediately struck them: first, it was written in Italian. This was most unusual when anything of importance was necessarily in Latin. In Italian even women could understand it.

And then, it was beautiful. The Florentines had a lively appreciation of beauty, and this fact both impressed them and made them pause. The words of the *Comedy* began to sound through the streets on the lips of a poetry-enchanted people. There were no social distinctions about this. Blacksmiths, wool-workers and rag-and-bone men murmured and sang it as well as priests and politicians and bankers.

Above all Giovanni Boccaccio was struck to the soul by the magical sound of the *Comedy*, and its author became the god of his life-long idolatry.

It seemed that Dante had made this journey of his in 1300, the year of the Jubilee, and had started to write about it *before* his exile. This much was clear from the story of the manuscript which was by now known to everybody.

Not long after the exile, Dante's wife Gemma had asked a nephew of hers to sort through a mass of old papers in the house, and while doing so the young man had come across a bundle which attracted his attention. The scrawl with which the top sheet was covered was practically illegible, but he managed to decipher something.

It seemed to be a story, told in the first person, about somebody who was lost in the middle of a dark wood. After a while this person came to the foot of a pleasant hill, bathed in the first rays of the sun, but was unable to climb it because of three beasts — a panther, a lion and a wolf — which barred his way. Then, when all seemed lost, a stranger appeared who turned out to be the great Latin poet, Virgil.

Virgil offered to take the writer on a terrible and mysterious journey into the other world, and after a brief discussion they set out upon this journey.

There were seven cantos in the bundles, 952 lines, divided into triplets, all inexorably linked together by rhyme, and although it was evidently unfinished, the whole thing was formed with a mathematically awesome proportion.

Considerably baffled, the young man took it to his aunt who recognised it as her husband's work. Under the circumstances, with four children to look after and Dante a figure of scorn throughout the city, it would have been understandable if she had thrown it into the fire. But she did not, and even Boccaccio, when later he wrote his biography, gave her grudging credit for saving a masterpiece.

She took it to one of her husband's poetical friends who was stunned by the composition. Nothing like it had ever been written before. It reared up from the lush, exquisitely cultivated landscape garden of the *dolce stil nuovo* like a massive rocky mountain impenetrably wrapped in cloud. The manuscript, said the poet, should be sent to Dante immediately.

It reached him while he was staying at the Malaspina castle, and he obviously continued it because the story now in circulation continued on through the bottom of Hell and out the other side.

And before long the Florentines were able to read the sequel, or rather sequels, for there were two, one telling the story of his long climb up Mount Purgatory, and the other of his dizzy flight through Paradise till he reached the ultimate and unrecordable beatific vision.

Manfred, who had died at Benevento, was at the very foot of Mount Purgatory on the terrace of the excommunicate (damned by Charles d'Anjou, but saved by God). And not far from him, among those who repented late, but still in time, was Charles d'Anjou himself. Also among the unshriven Dante saw Buonconte da Montefeltro, the Arezzo commander at Campaldino whose soul the angel was said to have wrested from the devil 'for a single little tear'. And Forese Donati, who had rioted with Dante among the fleshpots and in the stews, was higher up the mountain where the penitent gluttons are tormented by the sight of a fruit tree and a cascade of sparkling water of which they can never taste.

Then, having finally scaled Mount Purgatory to the very top, Dante at last met his Beatrice once again in the earthly Paradise from which man had first fallen. And from there he ascended with her to the great circles of Heaven where, in that of Venus, he had encountered that stupendous courtesan, Cunizza, eager yet in eternity to please and shining precisely there because in life she had been governed by that planet's influence.

In writing of Beatrice as the guide through Heaven who led him up through its wheeling spheres to the feet of the Virgin, Dante had unerringly fulfilled the promise made at the time of the *Vita Nuova*, 'to write of her what has never been written of any other woman'.

The Florentines had probably not yet heard the end of the story of Dante's journey through the three great kingdoms beyond the grave when the news reached them that he had embarked on his eternal sojourn beyond the grave.

The year was 1321. Boccaccio was eight years old, and Giotto was still engaged on the Bardi–Peruzzi frescoes in the Franciscan church of Santa Croce.

With news travelling slowly and erratically, it will have taken them a long time to piece together the story of the last years, particularly since, after the fiasco of Prince Henry, Dante's wanderings became vaguer than ever. 'Extremely poor,' said the early biographer, Leonardo Bruni, 'he passed the rest of his life in various places in Lombardy and Tuscany and Romagna, supported by various lords;' and during this time he learned by bitter experience, as he himself put it, how salt the bread of strangers is and how hard the climbing of other people's stairs.

During these years he had his last brush with the Florentines. Anxious to rally all the good will they could, they had offered a new amnesty to all the remaining exiles. But there were conditions. The penitent exiles, dressed in sack-cloth with a paper hat on their heads and carrying a candle, had to proceed to Saint John's, offer themselves symbolically to the Baptist and pay a fine.

Solicitous friends wrote to tell him of the offer, but the rearing pride of Dante, hard-pressed in exile, but never laid low, would not allow him to appear in the streets of Florence dressed like a clown.

'If this is the only way one may return to Florence,' he wrote in answer, 'then to Florence I shall never again return. Besides, what does it matter? Wherever I am, can I not contemplate the sun and the stars and meditate under the vault of Heaven on those truths which are so sweet to me, without first making myself contemptible, indeed abject, to the people and the entire city of Florence?'

It was about 1317 in Ravenna that Dante's journeyings, practically untraceable in the mists for so many years, brought him into a brief, lighted clearing before the end.

He was over fifty now, and the fierce strains which life had imposed on him were beginning to take their toll. Apart from acute poverty, he suffered from arthritis and various other disturbances. All earthly hopes had left him. He no longer even dreamed of a triumphant return to Florence. Most of his friends were dead, and those who were still alive were too far off to visit or be visited. There was nothing left for him but God and the *Comedy*.

He was invited to Ravenna as a teacher at the university there by Guido Novella, Count of Polenta. This Guido Novella was a man of culture who wrote verse himself, and the two of them often discussed poetry together. Moreover, he was a man of action which was pleasing to Dante who despised intellectuals who cut themselves off from the sweat and toil of everyday politics.

Guido had been a courageous and competent soldier as well as an efficient governor. He made use of all these experiences to take over command in Ravenna and administer the city's affairs wisely and well. He did not reign with anything like the splendour and pomp of Big Dog della Scala. He had a solid, unimposing palace in which he lived the life of an intellectual member of the middle classes, spending more time in his library than hunting or fighting.

Ravenna itself must have appealed to Dante, too. It was a small city, remote (largely thanks to the cautious policies of his host) from the ferocious bickerings and hackings of all the other cities Dante knew. Its origins were Etruscan. Its past had been glorious, but its present was tranquil. During the period of Byzantine domination it had been the great sea-port of northern Italy, but over the centuries as the sea withdrew further and further the star of Venice rose in the commercial–maritime sky until it outshone that of Ravenna altogether. It was prosperous enough, but memories were its second currency.

Two of Dante's sons, Pietro and Jacopo, joined him here together with his daughter Antonia, who became a nun at a convent in the town, significantly taking the name of Beatrice.

Here Dante lived and worked peacefully until the summer of 1321 when he was called on by his host to act as ambassador. For some while now the all-powerful state of Venice had been looking for an opportunity to wage war on Ravenna and take over her salt mines which were an irritating challenge to the Venetian monopoly of salt. The excuse came when the Ravennese unwisely became involved in a fight with some Venetian ships and killed some of their sailors.

War seemed imminent. But small, peaceful Ravenna could never hope to stand up to the vast power of Venice. So as soon as the Venetian lion roared, Guido Novella dispatched Dante, the most eloquent member of his court, to offer humble apologies and assurances that the guilty would be punished and such an incident would never occur again.

He became feverish on the outward journey, having caught malaria, but he was not the man to heed a temperature, and he went on. Venice did not declare war on Ravenna, so evidently the mission was a success, and Dante set out on the gruelling return journey under a blazing late-August sun, the fever now raging within him.

On the first day he crossed the lagoon by boat and then travelled by land as far as Loreto. By now he was seriously ill, but he insisted on going forward the next day. Perhaps some instinct drove him on to the one city that had ever given him peace.

He crossed the delta of the Po on one of the heavy barges used for ferrying and then went on to Pomposa where, like all travellers passing through in those days, he spent the night in the Benedictine abbey there. On the third day he reached Ravenna.

The news that he was gravely ill spread rapidly. His daughter, Sister Beatrice, tended him lovingly, but unavailingly. No one could halt the long decline into darkness. On the evening of 13 September the last agony set in. And during that night, in

Boccaccio's words, 'he gave up his troubled spirit to his Creator, and I do not doubt but that it was received into the arms of his most noble Beatrice with whom, in the presence of the supreme good, having left the miseries of this present life, he now dwells blissfully in that life where happiness never comes to an end.' He was fifty-six years old.

Everybody's immediate concern was the *Comedy*. He had worked on it up to almost the end of his life, and it was believed that he had finished it. His custom had been to send six or eight cantos at a time, as they were finished, to Big Dog della Scala 'whom he esteemed more than any other man'. And Big Dog then had copies made of them.

This custom had been continued up to but excluding the last thirteen cantos of *Paradise*. These cantos were the crown of the entire, stupendous fabric, containing, it was generally believed, Dante's vision of the Trinity. At all costs they had to be found. But the feverish searchings through his papers were in vain.

If they existed, the last thirteen cantos had disappeared.

It was Boccaccio who discovered and preserved the story of how they were found.

The search continued for eight months, he said, at the end of which the sons, Jacopo and Pietro, were urged by friends to finish the *Comedy* themselves. Reluctantly they set to work (the task might be compared with having to write the last movement of Beethoven's Ninth). But the project was brought to an abrupt and miraculous halt by a dream that Jacopo had one night.

In this dream Dante appeared to him, his face shining with light. Asked if he were alive, he replied, 'Yes, but with the true life and not this of ours.'

'Wherefore,' Boccaccio continued, 'he dreamed that he went on to ask whether he had finished his work before passing into the true life, and, if he had, where was the missing portion which they had never been able to find. To this he seemed, as before, to hear the answer, "Yes, I finished it." And then it seemed to him that he took him by the hand and led him into the room where he used to sleep when he lived in this life and, touching one of the walls with his hand, said, "Here is what you have been searching for for so long." And as soon as these words were spoken, it seemed to him that his sleep and Dante departed from him together.'

Although it was still the middle of the night, Jacopo could not wait to see whether the figure in his dream had been 'a true spirit or a false delusion', so he immediately went round to the house in which Dante had been living at the time of his death.

'And, having knocked up the present tenant and been let in by him, they went to the place indicated, and here found a mat fixed to the wall, which they had always seen hanging there in the past. This they gently lifted, and found in the wall a tiny window, which neither of them had ever seen before or known to be there. And within they found a quantity of written sheets, all mouldy with the dampness of the wall and ready to rot away if they had been left there any longer.

'When they had cleared off all the mould, they saw that the pages were numbered and, having placed them in order, they found they had recovered, altogether, the thirteen cantos that were lacking of the *Comedy*. Wherefore they copied them out rejoicing and, according to the custom of the author, sent them first of all to Master Cane, and afterwards reunited them to the unfinished work where they belonged.'

And so the epic poem 'to which both Heaven and Earth had put a hand' and which had taken so many years in the making was completed at last.

15

BANKER

While Giovanni Boccaccio was still a boy, and only two or three years after the death of Dante, his father became a partner with the merchant banking firm of Bardi for whom Giotto had just finished painting the story of Saint Francis in Santa Croce. So the family, the larger now by the birth of Giovanni's step-brother Jacopo, transferred from Certaldo to a large, gloomy house in Florence not far from the magnificent Bardi palaces.

Of all Florentine merchant families, the Bardis were the most clamorously successful. They dominated the European banking scene for a hundred years — from the middle of the thirteenth to the middle of the fourteenth century— and the story of Florence itself was profoundly influenced by them.

'At the time of the said war between the King of France and the King of England [the Hundred Years War],' wrote the chronicler Giovanni Villani, 'the Bardi and the Peruzzi acted as bankers for the King of England, and all the money and wool and everything that was of the King passed through their hands, and they paid all his costs and the pay of his soldiers and all that was needful to him; and the costs of the King were so much greater than his income that the Bardi, when he returned from war, found him to be in their debt for more than £135,000.'

Having attained such heights in the banking world, Boccaccio senior was determined that his son should follow him. 'His father,' wrote a contemporary, 'so willing it, and compelling him from motives of profit, he was obliged to apply himself to the abacus.'

So it was that before he was thirteen Giovanni unwillingly

started work as an apprentice or office boy with the Bardi bank, for the moment unpaid, but destined for a partnership like his father with a sliding salary starting with the equivalent of about £5,000 and rising to something like £50,000.

There were some disadvantages, however, to a senior position with the Bardis. There was no welfare or union protection, and illness meant an immediate salary reduction, followed by dismissal if it were protracted. Furthermore, partners were obliged to pass to the bank any presents they might receive in the course of their work, and were not to have mistresses or to gamble.

Nevertheless, if he could only overcome the rooted aversion he had for all forms of money making, Giovanni could look forward to a long, prosperous and respectable career as a merchant banker.

The Florence he saw about him as he walked to and from his office stool was not so much a beautiful as a war-like one. A new circle of walls had been finished and three massive fortified gates had gone up. The palace of the Signoria, the seat of government, had not long been finished, and its grim assymetrical outline which reared up over the entire city seemed to express the spirit of Florence.

A new bell had just been installed in this palace, and it was considered to be the most perfect bell ever made. It had been hung 'with fine and subtle skill, so that two men could move it, and once it had been moved only one could ring a peal whereas before twelve men had not been sufficient'.

This bell was looked after by a communal bell-ringer who lived in a little wooden hut in the tower and had a special uniform with a bell on it bearing the red lily of Florence. The sound of the new bell in the Signoria went out for thirteen miles about the city which meant that it was well within hearing of the city's enemies.

For once again things were looking bad for Florence. A league of various city states was threatening her liberty if not her existence. With extreme reluctance the Florentines had turned for help to Robert of Anjou, King of Naples. They were reluctant because calling in outsiders had always been fatal in the past; and, indeed, it was to be no less so on this occasion, but the situation was a desperate one.

Robert sent his son, Charles, Duke of Calabria, who arrived in Florence on 30 July 1326, accompanied by his wife and a crowd of great lords, many of them French. Giovanni Boccaccio said that he was part of the enormous crowd which thronged the streets to welcome him. The occasion was spectacular. Charles was escorted by 1,910 knights, 317 of whom had gold spurs, and the court baggage was borne on 1,500 mules.

The Florentines elected him 'Lord Regent, Defender and Protector' of their city, and bitterly regretted it at once. Charles halted free elections, abolished constitutional guarantees and made incessant demands on the city treasury. He also sent for reinforcements of 1,000 knights from neighbouring cities all of whom, like his own court, lived at the expense of the Florentines.

Indeed, the bills were the worst part of this bad bargain, for Charles kept very high court indeed with his sixteen-year-old wife, Marie de Valois. He employed 160 personal attendants for himself and fifty-eight for her as well as sixty armed bodyguards, four clowns, two doctors, a surgeon, four private musicians and an astrologer. For a single fur robe Charles had made for himself 1,034 squirrel pelts were used. Tennis, imported from France, was all the rage at court. It was played indoors, usually in the evening, with goat-skin balls stuffed with feathers.

What with tennis and other delights, the Florentines soon discovered that Charles and his knights were not exactly spoiling for battle. Their presence rendered the city itself safe enough for the moment, but the marauding army still pillaged and looted in the surrounding countryside, and the defender and protector did nothing to stop it.

Ten months after his arrival in Florence, the Duke of Calabria was recalled by his father who needed assistance in Naples. He left in as great pomp as he had come, and when he had gone the Florentines reckoned that he had cost them 900,000 gold florins. The best that could be said was that much of this had been spent within the city, but in the meantime there wasn't enough money in the treasury to pay the civil servants.

But with Charles gone, the tide suddenly and unexpectedly turned in the favour of the Florentines. For some while now they had been increasingly menaced by Castruccio Castracani, Lord of Lucca and one of the great condottieri of the age, whose supreme aim was the conquest of Florence. And it was beginning to appear dangerously as though he might achieve it. Already, three years before in 1325, he had conquered nearby Pistoia and inflicted a painful defeat on the Florentine army. Now it seemed that he was free to come and go as he wished in Tuscany and that the conquest of the unconquerable Florence itself was only a question of time.

Castruccio's character is shrewdly caught in an anecdote of the period. One day he sent a servant ahead of him to prepare food in a castle he had recently captured. On arrival there the servant saw, among the coats-of-arms on the wall, the lily of Florence, and he immediately struck it through with his lance. Then, when Castruccio arrived, he said to him, 'See, my lord, how I have dealt with the arms of those traitor Florentines.'

Castruccio said nothing at the time, but stored the episode away in his mind. Some days later they met a contingent of the Florentine army with an imposing-looking infantryman in the front line bearing a shield with the Florentine lily on it.

'When Castruccio saw that this man was in the vanguard of the attack, he called his servant who had so gallantly fought against the wall and said to him, "Come here — some days ago you gave such fine blows to the lily on the wall that you altogether undid it. Now go forthwith and conquer that one." '

On learning that the alternative was hanging from the nearest tree, the servant attacked as he had been told and was instantly killed 'with a lance that went through him from one side to the other'.

'May you all learn,' said Castruccio, turning impassively to those about him, 'to fight with the living and not the dead.'

In 1327 another Holy Roman Emperor, Ludovic of Bavaria, appeared over the Alps, and it was to help defend them against him as well as against Castruccio that the Florentines had called for the help of King Robert of Naples. But indirectly it was the arrival of Ludovic that saved the day for them. Because of the danger he represented, Charles, Duke of Calabria, had left Florence to shore up the Neapolitan defences; and to attend his coronation Castruccio now left Tuscany for Rome.

Swiftly taking advantage of his absence, the Florentines immediately re-captured Pistoia. When the news reached him

Castruccio set out to return, but he was struck down by malaria on the way.

'And shortly before his death, knowing himself to be dying, he said to his closest friends, "I can see myself dying, and once I am dead you will see everything fall to pieces." '

So it was, as far as the anti-Florentine league was concerned. As for the Florentines, 'as soon as they could believe that he was dead', they went wild with joy.

Just before this triumph, while Charles was still in Florence, Boccaccio's father was appointed director of the Bardi branch in Naples. He set off there by himself and then sent for his elder son to join him. Delighted at the prospect of escaping from his stepmother, Boccaccio left Florence.

He arrived in Naples after a journey of two weeks, took one look at the ripe southern beauty of the girls, the dark and suggestive little alleys, the rich, flaunting costumes, and at once recognised that he had come to paradise.

Naples was even older than Rome itself. It had been founded as a Greek colony about six centuries before Christ. The Romans took it in 326 B.C. and it beguiled their intellectuals, their patricians and even some of their emperors.

Nero was the one who loved it most. Having planned an opera tour of Greece, with himself as the star, he decided to hold a dress rehearsal in the city. It lasted uninterruptedly for six days and included a series of sumptuous banquets. The Neapolitans flocked enthusiastically to this spectacle which had just the sort of extravagance that delighted them. Half way through there was an earthquake which spread panic through the audience but left the Emperor singing imperturbably on. It was all very Neapolitan.

The Naples Boccaccio now saw was 'happy, peaceful, abundant and magnificent' on the surface, and swarming and pullulating with black misery below. But the sheer beauty of the place was unaffected by this and it enraptured him. The gulf had diaphanous, unreal colours on which the boats seemed to hang as though in the air and the islands turned into crystal at sunset. The slopes of Vesuvius were covered with the most fertile orchards and vineyards in Italy. There was an almost Oriental atmosphere about the place created by the ships which sailed daily into its port, bringing with them spices and the most fantastic tales. And although the dark back streets and alleys were dangerous after nightfall, they nevertheless rustled invitingly in the hot evening air.

The life of the streets was inexhaustible. There were sword-swallowers and snake-charmers, story-tellers and ballad singers with their audiences higgledy-piggledy about them among the innumerable stalls. Street sellers pushed their way through the swarming, squabbling sea of humanity.

And everywhere there swarmed the *scugnizzi* — the gutter urchins — an eternal feature of the Neapolitan scene, stealing, playing, mocking and chanting.

Then, even lower in the age scale, there were the smallest children and the babies — 'the creatures' as they are still called — omnipresent in Naples, the capital of copulation, seized with a wild zest for the creation of new life, whatever horrors might be inflicted on it later.

Food, spicy and aphrodisiac, was on sale up and down all the streets, including the greatest of Neapolitan gastronomic creations and one of the oldest delicacies of mankind, said to date back to before the introduction of plates when it was evolved as a sort of edible plate — the pizza.

Removed from this swarming Naples of the streets was royal Naples where Robert of Anjou lived with his court. This little kingdom without the city walls and overlooking the sea was a perfect world in miniature, one square kilometre large. In its elegance, it was utterly dissimilar from the city it belonged to. Instead of narrow alleys, it had broad avenues. Instead of crowded squares there were formal French gardens.

For Boccaccio this little world was still remote, but another Florentine was working busily at the heart of it. Following the royal summons, Giotto, now in his sixties, had left Florence yet again and set to work in the Anjou kingdom where he quickly formed a warm and intimate friendship with the King. Robert of Anjou was now moving peacefully and opulently towards the end of his reign. He had not always been a wise king nor a virtuous one, as various bastards still witnessed. But he had known how to govern the patchwork kingdom happily, and at the same time to amass great wealth.

Now in old age, he was a model of the sage and pious monarch. He had a passion for theology, and indeed Dante had referred indirectly to him when he had spoken of an age which makes kings out of those intended for preachers. Robert, in fact, went preaching throughout his kingdom and delivered one lengthy sermon before an entire convent of the nuns of Saint Clare.

This was the man with whom Giotto had embarked on a five-year friendship. The King, it was said, enjoyed above all things watching Giotto at work and listening to him talk. 'And Giotto,' reported Vasari, 'who was always ready with a joke or a witty response, would hold the King's interest with his painting on the one hand and a stream of amusing conversation on the other.'

The air of Naples, however, must have gone to his head for he allowed himself to be involved in a controversy that was raging at the time on the subject of poverty of all things. He even sat down solemnly, a medieval multi-millionaire, and composed a 'Song on Poverty'.

During his five years in Naples he is said to have painted 'many scenes from the Old and New Testaments in several of the convent chapels', including some of the Apocalypse, proposed to him as a theme so legend has it, by Dante during some meeting in his exile.

Not a brush-stroke of all this work survived. Indeed, if one thing is more surprising than the amount of work by Giotto and his school which lasted, it is the amount which vanished. This lost world of Giotto includes several entire series of frescoes.

While Giotto was chatting with the King and painting, Boccaccio was living in the streets of Naples and dying — in all but the merely physical sense — in the offices of the Bardi bank which were in the busy commercial quarter of Naples near the port. Working hours had to be respected, and the atmosphere was rigidly, tediously Florentine.

And so it went on for two years, with the bank peremptorily exerting one set of claims, and life another. Then in 1329 Robert, the King, made Boccaccio senior one of his own treasury officials. For Giovanni, now nearly seventeen, it must have seemed as though the impossible had happened. The doors of the court were flung open and he was made free of its delights just at the age when he could make the riotous best of them.

At about the same time as Giovanni entered the court of

Naples, Giotto left it and set off once again northwards towards Florence and what was to be in many ways the most sensational job of his career.

16

TOWER

Giotto returned to a Florence that was, like himself, richer than ever. Internecine conflict had not ceased, but it was subtler and less bloody than in the days of Corso Donati. The more gentlemanly, but none the less deadly, rivalries that prevailed now were among the great bankers, the new overlords of the city.

There were eighty banks there now, making Florence the financial capital of the known world. France and England depended entirely upon loans from Florentine bankers, and the city's annual income was greater than that of the whole of England under Elizabeth I. And the people who were making all this money were pouring it back in the form of hospitals, schools, churches, painting and sculpture which they commissioned.

Then suddenly all this prosperity was checked by yet another calamity, this time a natural one. It struck in 1333 when Boccaccio, now twenty years old, was still plunging like a porpoise in the delights of Naples.

'On All Saints' Day,' wrote Villani, 'the city of Florence being strong and in more happy and contented state than it had ever been since 1300, it began to rain in and about the city and in the Alps and the mountains, and so it continued without stop for four days and four nights, the rain pouring down more and more heavily and beyond all its normal usage, so it seemed as though the cataracts of heaven had been opened.

'And with the said rain there was continuous and loud and terrible thunder and lightning, and many thunderbolts fell, so that all the people lived in great fear, continually ringing the bells of the churches throughout the city until the water began to rise.

'And in all the houses they beat continually on basins and cooking pots, with loud cries calling *misericordia, misericordia* to God for those who were in danger. And people fled from house to house and from roof to roof, making bridges from one house to another, so that there was such great noise and tumult you could scarcely hear the thunder.'

It was the worst flood in the city's history. The Arno broke its banks and flooded all the countryside about, and by 4 November it was so swollen that it smashed a great breach in the city walls. In St John's the water rose up to the top of the pillars. There was a death toll of about 300, though at the time so great was the panic that they estimated it at 3,000.

'And to estimate the damage suffered by the Florentines,' said Villani, 'I, who saw these things, could name no sum, but such ruin of bridges and walls and streets was wrought in the city alone that to repair it cost more than 150,000 gold florins.'

The last remains of Roman Florence disappeared in this flood, including — and the symbolism would have escaped nobody — the statue of the god of war, Mars, at the foot of which the young Buondelmonte had been murdered more than a century before.

Fire had always been another major hazard, and it still was when flood did not render it impossible. The Florentines combated it by the formation of an official fire brigade. It had its own tower and evolved a sophisticated fire-fighting technique with ladders, hooks, axes and buckets. There was a fire chief, forty skilled firemen, twenty unskilled helpers and two lantern bearers. They were divided into four groups for the four quarters of the city, and the firemen wore iron helmets and a uniform with an axe on the front and the coat-of-arms of the quarter they belonged to on the back. The helpers just had buckets back and front.

Crime, which used to sweep the city by night, was now suppressed by a regular nocturnal police force of 600, working in simple shifts of 300 one night and 300 the next. The guilds had their police, too, mainly to reduce the large number of thefts and stop the illicit gambling which went on in the backs of shops.

A special morals magistrature had been set up to deal with vice. Its main function was to fix tariffs and establish those parts of the city where prostitutes might or might not solicit. Penalties for contravention of the decrees laid down by this magistrature included being whipped naked and being lowered three times into the Arno by the public executioner.

Architecturally, the city was taking on a new aspect, especially in the new squares like those in front of Santa Maria Novella and Santa Croce where the closed, squat buildings of the thirteenth century were giving way to edifices with the sweeping lines of the Gothic. And glass was beginning to appear in the windows, small round pieces of it held together with lead.

For a long while now the Florentines had had a dream of marble. They wanted to build for their Cathedral the mightiest and most beautiful bell-tower that had ever existed. It was, they stated specifically, to outdo in height and splendour the supreme achievements of the Greeks and the Romans at their greatest. It was a very Florentine ambition.

There was, of course, only one man who could direct such a project. By now, Giotto, back from Naples, was full of years as well as honours, but he was also extremely hale. In April 1334 he was named 'master and governor' of the city's building works, which meant that he was responsible not only for the Cathedral and its tower, but also for the city walls, bridges and fortifications.

'Desiring,' said the official decree, 'that the building works in progress in the city of Florence should proceed in honourable and decorous fashion, and bearing in mind that this cannot be unless some man of skill and renown be nominated to direct them, and considering that no one in the entire world can be found more competent in these and other things than Master Giotto of Bondone, painter of Florence, who is worthy to be esteemed in his own land as a great master and to be held dear in the said city, and so that he may be able to reside permanently therein in order that many may profit from his science and doctrine and that he may bring honour to the city itself . . . ' for all these motives Giotto was installed in the highest office of its nature that Florence had to offer.

It was exactly what he needed, for by now he had painted himself out. On his shoulders he had carried the art of painting into a new age. He had travelled tirelessly from city to city all over Italy, painting whatever was asked of him, and in the process winning more wealth and honour than any artist before him could ever have dreamed of. But now the seemingly inexhaustible flood of painting had dried up. He wanted a new challenge. The tower gave it to him.

At the age of sixty-seven his energies could leap up again with the driving vigour which had executed the huge frescoes in Assisi, covered the walls and ceiling of the Scrovegni chapel, turned the Bardi and Peruzzi chapels into Aladdin's caves of glowing life. But the material he was to work in was no longer paint, frail in the face of time, but marble which could hold its own against the centuries.

Giotto was a practical man who believed in exploiting any skill he might have to fill his coffers, but even he must have been exhilarated at the prospect of rearing up into the sky of Florence a tower that would be the synthesis of all that was painting, sculpture and architecture.

It was fitting, too, that his career which had started in the Baptistery at the side of his master, Cimabue, should now, towards the end, lead him back where he had come from — for the Baptistery, the Cathedral and the Bell-Tower are the trinity of Florence. Their story mirrors the city's.

The Baptistery is the oldest. Its origins are lost in time, and it stands upon the bones of even older ancestors, for excavations have revealed the remains of a palaeochristian church and, below that again, the traces of a Roman building with its mosaics. The Baptistery itself was built in about the eleventh or twelfth centuries and dedicated to Saint John the Baptist. It was a squat, uncompromising, octagonal building with no pretensions to grandeur, its three doors pointing directly towards three points of the compass and, Florentine affluence still being in the distant future, its outer walls were built of simple sandstone.

Its magnificent trappings came to it slowly over the centuries. The white marble of Carrara and the green marble of Prato which now cover the external walls had only just begun to go up when Dante saw the building for the last time. And it had to wait until the middle of the fifteenth century for its eastern door by Lorenzo Ghiberti which Michelangelo called 'the gate of Paradise'.

In fact, it did not start life as a baptistery at all, but as the Cathedral of Florence, only changing its role when the population explosion demanded a larger building. But for long after that all Florentines considered it as the focal point of their city, and in an age when churches were as much the houses of man as of God and used for political meetings, conspiracies, places of refuge, gossip centres and lovers' lanes, it was the true centre of Florence on which all lines converged. When Dante in exile looked back on his city, the building that always reared up in his mind amid the hostile towers was his 'beautiful St John'.

So the Baptistery united Florence even in disunity. This life and the next both took their starting point from it, and the Florentines were great believers in both.

When the Baptistery became too small to serve as a cathedral, its place was taken by the church opposite named after Santa Reparata, a young girl martyr of the primitive church, for whom the Florentines had a great devotion, attributing to her their salvation from an invasion of Ostrogoths in the early phases of the city's history. But scarcely a century went by before this, too, became inadequate.

Besides, there was a question of prestige to be considered. All the rival — and, of course, lesser — city states possessed magnificent cathedrals. Could Florence be left lagging behind? The order for a new cathedral went out in 1294 in much the same terms as the order was to go out forty years later for the bell-tower. It was to be 'such that it is impossible to imagine one greater or more beautiful created by the industry and power of men.'

'In the said year of 1294,' it was reported, 'the city of Florence being in a very peaceful way, the citizens agreed to re-build the main church which was roughly constructed, poor and small for such a great city, and they ordered it should be increased in size and moved back from the Baptistery and all covered in marble with sculpted figures.'

Obviously the architect had to be the best available, and so they went to Arnolfo di Cambio who was held to be the greatest living master of stone. Having been born nearly thirty years before Giotto in 1240 he was fifty-four at the time of the Florentine summons and at the height of his powers. As a young man of twenty-five he had made a spectacular début by collaborating with the great Nicola Pisano on one of the two stupendously sculpted pulpits at Pisa, and later, like Giotto, he had been called to work in Rome as the leader of his profession.

One of the first problems was to make room for the new cathedral, as every inch of space in the city centre was occupied. So a large number of houses had to be knocked down before they could even start. One family which owned property there, the Bischeri, demanded such exorbitant compensation that the government refused to pay. It seemed as though the whole stupendous project was to be held up for a handful of houses. Then miraculously and — so it is said — entirely by accident a fire started and consumed those very houses, leaving the Bischeri without a single florin in compensation. Ever since in Florence, 'to do a Bischeri' has meant to act foolishly in business.

If the Bischeri were hostile to the building of the Cathedral, they were the only family in the city who were. For everybody else, the building of it became a corporate crusade. All the fierce, concentrated Florentine pride of city was directed onto the project, and it could be dangerous for any outsider who did not share it, or at least pretend to.

A Veronese who was foolish enought to lift his eyebrows at the luxurious plans and ask where all the money was coming from was at once clapped into prison and kept there for two months. It is said that before letting him go they took him under armed escort and showed him the huge coffers of the Florentine exchequer overflowing with golden florins.

No means of raising money was overlooked. Pope Boniface even responded handsomely with 3,000 florins. Usurers were promised indulgences in exchange for contributions. Every citizen paid special cathedral taxes. But the direct taxation was nothing to the indirect taxation. It was impossible to carry out the smallest operation without paying a cathedral tax on it. The only person not taxed was the architect, Arnolfo.

Florentines ran death-bed races with each other to leave large sums for the Cathedral, and many more did not wait until the end, but voluntarily emptied, or at any rate lightened their purses for the greater glory of God.

Arnolfo died in 1301, the grimmest year in Florentine history when the Black–White conflict reached its bloody climax, when Dante served his ill-fated two months as prior, when Charles de Valois pretended not to see as the Blacks ripped Florence to pieces. Already the walls and scaffolding of the Cathedral rose up superbly in the midst of the human tragedy.

The death of Arnolfo brought a temporary halt to the project, and the tremendous emotional momentum which had swept it forward lost strength as the Florentines became entirely absorbed in politics. But interest was re-awoken with Giotto's appointment in April 1334, just six months after the catastrophic flood. However, rather than continue with the work on the Cathedral façade, he preferred to concentrate all his energy on the tower, and he prepared a design.

This design was discovered in Siena in 1885 and it shows that Giotto intended to produce a tower of truly colossal proportions in comparison with the one that was finally built. What is today called Giotto's Campanile is 265 feet high and is flat on top. What Giotto originally had in mind was an edifice surmounted by a spire with an angel at the summit, and from the ground to the top of the angel's head it would have measured 355 feet, an achievement that would have satisfied the wildest Florentine pretensions to glory.

The foundation stone was laid on 9 July 1334. They had dug to about 40 feet, excavated the water and gravel and then laid about 24 feet of ballast, filling up the remaining 16 feet with masonry. The Bishop laid the first stone in the presence of Giotto and both the ecclesiastical and civil hierarchies of Florence.

Unlike any previous project of Giotto's, this of the tower was dogged by criticism and misadventure. An anonymous Florentine commentator said that Giotto 'designed and supervised the marble tower of Santa Reparata in Florence, a most notable tower and of great cost'. (Like all Florentines he continued to use the old name of Santa Reparata instead of the new one of Santa Maria del Fiore.) 'But,' the commentator adds, 'he made two mistakes: the base was not big enough and the tower was too narrow.' Giotto was so overwhelmed with sorrow at this, he adds, that he took sick and died. But such drastic remorse was not in keeping with Giotto's sturdy, sceptical philosophy.

Criticism went on over the years, the burden of it being that Giotto was a painter and not an architect. But the Florentines were too hard-headed to have made a mistake like that. They had appointed Giotto director of public works, and the tower was not the only project he was responsible for. Apart from bridges, walls and fortifications, the city had by no means recovered from the flood of the previous year. It took six months just to clear the streets of mud. So it was not the moment to put an amateur in charge of public works.

Two hundred years later, Lorenzo Ghiberti — sculptor, artist, architect, goldsmith, art historian and creator of the Gate of Paradise in the Baptistery — said that the first stories carved at the base of the tower were designed and executed by Giotto himself. This is borne out by Antonio Pucci, bell-ringer, town-crier and poet in Florence at the time the tower was being built. Giotto, he said, carried the project so far ahead as to do the first carvings 'in fine style'. These carvings show man learning how to plough and breaking in the horse.

But in spite of his age and the importance attached to the tower, Giotto was not allowed to dedicate himself to it entirely. In 1335 Azzone Visconti asked the Florentines to lend him Giotto in Milan.

By now, like it or not, Giotto was a great old man, and so the negotiations were conducted by the city of Florence itself, and the venerable master was finally dispatched. He spent the best part of a year in Milan and apparently did some allegories and historical portraits. Not a brush-stroke of them remains.

When he returned to Florence, he was no longer able to carve or even mount the scaffolding, and he could do little but enjoy, or at any rate endure, the glory which lapped all about him. His work was venerated throughout the length and breadth of Italy; his pupils preached the gospel according to Giotto whereby the art of painting itself had been resurrected from the dead; his native city honoured him as her greatest son.

The old man's tranquillity was a little disturbed by an invitation from the Pope to go to Avignon and fresco the bare walls of the huge papal palace there with the lives and deaths of the martyrs. He did not exactly refuse — it was not in his nature, and even on the brink of seventy the lure of a vast fee tempted him — but he procrastinated until death called a final halt to the project.

It came to him in Florence on 8 January 1337. The government decreed that after solemn public honour had been paid to him, he should be buried in the Cathedral, an honour quite without precedent for a painter. And indeed, wrote Vasari, 'he was buried in Santa Maria del Fiore on the left as you go into the church where there is a slab of white marble raised in memory of such a great man.' But for all Vasari's precision, nobody has ever managed to find the tomb.

On Giotto's death his assistant, Andrea Pisano, took his place as master of works. By then the tower was some twelve feet above the ground. Pisano took it up about the same height again. Then the work was briefly directed by Giotto's own pupil, Taddeo Gaddi. But the man who took it all the way up to the top was a certain Francesco Talenti.

Yet, all over the world people speak only of Giotto's tower. And it is right they should do so. Not only were the inspiration and the basic design his, but the whole edifice rests on his foundation and base. And in six centuries it has not shown a single crack or budged a centimetre.

17

FLAME

For all the preaching of its monarch, the Anjou court at Naples was among the most dissolute in Europe, and it was consequently the happiest of hunting grounds for Giovanni Boccaccio who had, in his own words, 'belonged to Venus since childhood'.

He was young and good-looking, tall with a generously sensual mouth, bright eyes and a dimple in his chin. His nature was spontaneous and generous; he was amusing, a brilliant talker, a *raconteur* and above all a poet. And if the hunt was animated, it was never prolonged. One of his earliest writings, in fact, is an intoxicated paean of praise to the most noted beauties of Naples entitled 'The Hunt of Diana'.

These adventures were the small change of court life at Naples, but Giovanni was shortly to embark on one that was a great deal more. It was to raise him to the heights of bliss and plummet him to the depths of misery. There was just a brief period, however, before he set eyes on the cause of it all, when he was able to enjoy the delights of Neapolitan high society unalloyed by jealousy and all the other passions she was to arouse in him.

Not all these delights were carnal. The university and the royal library opened up an endless sea of learning into which he plunged enthusiastically. Literature, astronomy, philosophy, the sciences, mythology, astrology — he was indiscriminately hungry for them all. He also started to learn Greek which was to be a lifelong delight for him.

But the headiest intellectual joy of all came from the poet

Cino da Pistoia who taught at the university. As well as being a poet, Cino was a celebrated jurist, but what elevated him to an almost supernatural level in Boccaccio's eyes was that he had been a friend of Dante. Boccaccio had heard something of the *Comedy* in Florence, but he had probably not glimpsed more than fragments of the great mosaic. Now he was able to read it all for himself under the guidance of someone who knew his way about the three mysterious kingdoms.

But of course there had to be a flaw in all this happiness. Boccaccio's father, who disapproved violently of his son's literary-intellectual ideas, kept his nose firmly to the grindstone of prosaic business activity. 'From childhood on,' wrote Boccaccio junior, 'my father forced me in every possible way to become a man of trade. I had scarcely entered upon my adolescence when, after I had acquired the elements of arithmetic, he sent me as a pupil to a very important merchant with whom for six years I did nothing but waste time, which you can never have back again.'

After a while, however, even Boccaccio's father realised it was a futile endeavour, but he still would not admit he was beaten. 'It having been made abundantly plain that I was more suited for literary studies, my father himself commanded that I should pass to the study of canon law so as to become rich. And so, under the tutelage of another famous master, for almost the same amount of time I worked in vain.'

But inwardly Boccaccio was stubborn. 'My soul,' he said, 'loathed these things, and the counsels of my tutors, the authority of my father and the reproaches of my friends all went for nothing.'

There was as much humility in Boccaccio as there was genius. Dante and Giotto had a very shrewd idea of their own worth. Not Boccaccio. He never thought he had achieved anything worth doing. Writing of this period in his full maturity he said, 'I do not doubt that I really would have become a good poet, if my father had let me when I was the right age for such studies. Instead he forced me first into a money-making trade and then into money-making studies, with the result that now I am neither a merchant nor an expert in canon law. And I have missed the chance of becoming a great poet.'

On the Saturday of Easter Week 1336, when Giovanni was

twenty-three came the thunderbolt. Having gone to the church of St Laurence near where he was living he first saw the girl who was to cause him such extremes of bliss and despair. And he was never really to get over it.

Writing of his birth, Boccaccio transformed his mother from superfluous widow into a French princess, and in the same way, describing this affair, he presented the girl in church as a countess, the illegitimate daughter of King Robert of Anjou.

On the death of her putative father she was said to have been put into a convent from which she escaped and made a rich, but unhappy marriage. At the time Giovanni first saw her, she was one of the greatest beauties of Neapolitan high society, but intelligent with it, surrounded by an army of admirers, having acquired to perfection the art of holding at arm's length without discouraging.

Her name, it seemed, was Maria d'Aquino (her husband belonging to the same family as St Thomas Aquinas), but Boccaccio always wrote of her as Fiammetta, or Flame.

His account of the affair, called *Elegy for Madonna Fiammetta* was written when he was back in prosaic, money-making, aggressive Florence, yearning sadly for the scented gardens of Naples. In it the whole thing is described from her point of view, not his, and one of the most detailed scenes is her account of their first meeting in church.

'That day,' she said, 'was particularly solemn for the whole world, so I dressed myself carefully with gold-shining robes and adorned myself with skilful hand and prepared myself to go to the august ceremony.' And once there, 'ancient custom and my noble heritage reserved for me one of the foremost places among the other women'.

Eyeing the girls in church has always been a great Italian sport. Much of Dante's observation of Beatrice and the 'screen' loves was conducted during Mass. And nine years before Boccaccio's fatal encounter, Petrarch had first seen his Laura on Good Friday in the church of Saint Clare at Avignon. So it was now.

'Not only the eyes of the men turned to look at me,' said Fiammetta, 'but even those of the women, just as though Venus or Minerva, never before seen by them, were in that place where I had newly arrived.'

All the lesser beauties were forgotten as the young men 'grouped about me and surrounded me like a crown, and, talking among themselves of my beauty, drew the conclusion of their praises in almost identical words.'

Fiammetta pretended to notice none of this, being absorbed in prayer. 'While in this way I stayed — glancing a little at a few, stared at much by many — thinking of how my beauty ensnared others, it happened that I myself was wretchedly taken. I saw a youth right opposite me, alone and leaning against a marble column. And moved by inscrutable destiny I set myself to studying him and his way as I have never before studied another.

'He was of exceedingly fine appearance, most pleasing in his ways and honest in his dress, and the soft and curly hair upon his cheeks bore pleasing witness of his young manhood. With my eyes more firmly fixed in his than was their wont, it seemed to me that I saw written in them the words, "Oh, lady, you alone are our beatitude!"

'Truly, if I were to say these words did not please me, I should be lying; indeed, so greatly did they please me that they drew a gentle sigh from my breast, bearing with it the words, "And you are mine!" '

She was exasperated by the other young men who crowded between her and Giovanni. 'Some of them, thinking that my gaze fell upon them, perhaps believed themselves to be loved by me.' Not a word had passed between her and Giovanni, but by the time the Mass was over a firm understanding had been established.

The siege of Fiammetta lasted for six months and the ammunition was verse. One day the two of them went in a party to visit a convent outside Naples. The talk fell on a famous love story of the time, *Floire et Blanchefleur*, which had been spread by the French troubadours. It was an affecting story of young love and fidelity, the sort of story that held a great appeal for Fiammetta. It was such a pity, she said, that it was only passed from mouth to mouth and not put down on paper.

That was more than enough for Boccaccio, and as he wrote the story he read it aloud to her, noticing that she grew perceptibly more tender towards him as he did so.

The trouble was the husband. 'If that serpent who guards the treasure for which Love has made me so eager would lower his head just a little, I believe that skilful dealing would bring some solace to my tears.'

Fiammetta was carefully watched, and any scandal, with people of such high station involved, could have been dangerous for Giovanni who was still, after all, only a bank clerk. On the other hand, Fiammetta was no fool and it was certainly not her first affair; things could be arranged if she so wished.

When summer came she went off with the rest of the *jeunesse dorée* of Naples to that part of the Amalfi coast beyond the little Anjou kingdom where the rich and the noble disported themselves during the season.

She warned him not to follow her for fear of arousing scandal, but he disregarded the warning, and it was there, in the little fishing village of Baia, that Fiammetta gracefully and enchantingly fell to Giovanni.

Exultantly reeling off the names of thirty-two mountains, Boccaccio says that none of them had ever, with their shade, brought such gladness to their shepherds as had come to him in Baia 'where Love was so benevolent as to bring solace to all my burning'.

Literature being the means which had brought about the conquest, he continued to pour out words in the hope of consolidating it. He wrote a *Troilus and Cressida* and a monumental history of Theseus in 10,000 lines.

But not all the books in the world could hold Fiammetta. He had scarcely embarked on the first story he wrote for her when he began to have doubts which quickly grew into torments. If she could betray her husband, he asked himself as many had done before him in similar situations, could she not also betray him? She could. He came to loathe those delightful little spots along the bay of Naples where he had wooed and won Fiammetta. Venus, he said, had such unbridled licence in them that a girl who arrived as Lucretia went away as Cleopatra. Who could be a better judge than he?

With increasing suspicion, jealousy and bitterness the affair staggered on for three years. When it ended, Giovanni was overcome with rage and anguish. 'Liar!' he shrieked at Love, 'disloyal and treacherous, fraud-monger, murderer, thief, brigand, cruel tyrant, forsworn assassin!' Never again, he swore, would he raise his eyes to a woman, 'when I think what one has done to me'. But of course he did.

Affairs of the heart were not the only ones that were going badly. The mighty Florentine banking house of Bardi, on which the family fortunes depended, was swaying dangerously in the high financial winds. It had loaned too heavily to Edward III of England, and all the signs were that it was toppling helplessly into a bankruptcy that would make the whole of Europe tremble. And in fact, shortly after this, both the Bardi and the Peruzzi banks crashed, as a result of which, said Villani, 'our city of Florence was grievously shaken'.

In the meantime this meant for Giovanni the end of court life. His father, who had been busy accumulating property, now had to sell it to pay off debts, and at the same time, probably foreseeing imminent disaster, he left the Bardi bank and returned to Florence.

Giovanni stayed on in Naples for a while, trying to re-capture the lost dream. But, finding it hopeless, he too abandoned it, still goaded to distraction by desire for Fiammetta which could never find satisfaction again. The year was 1340 and he was now in his late twenties. The Neapolitan adventure had lasted for thirteen years.

In spite of all the changes and improvements that had been made in Florence, the returning Giovanni looked upon it more sourly than ever. He was still obsessed by the Florentine merchants— 'utterly ignorant, knowing nothing more than the number of steps from their shops or warehouses to their homes — as if knowledge served no other purpose than to cheat or make money'.

And the atmosphere at home did nothing to improve matters. 'Nobody laughs there,' he wrote, 'the dark, dumb, melancholy house holds and receives me against my will.' Nor had the years softened him towards his father who presented 'the cruel and horrible sight of a cold, harsh, mean old man'.

No wonder that his thoughts and dreams went increasingly from Florence, 'so abundantly furnished with proud, grasping and jealous folk', back to the 'happy, peaceful, abundant city of Naples' from which he had torn himself so reluctantly.

Boccaccio's low opinion of the city was in no way improved by events. Things had been going badly and so, heedless of all past experience, it was decided once again to call in 'a strong man' to raise political and military prestige.

This time it was Walter of Brienne, nominal Duke of Athens, who had by a sinister coincidence been in Florence sixteen years before as right-hand man to Charles de Valois when Corso Donati's rape of the city had been so studiously ignored. This Walter was 'small in stature, ugly and bearded, looking more Greek than French, and he was shrewd and cunning'.

He was shrewd and cunning enough to penetrate the safeguards with which the Florentines had hoped to protect their democracy. Their intention had been to appoint him 'Keeper and Protector of the State, Captain of War and of the City Defence' for one year only. But during the installation ceremony 'certain carders and meanly born persons and certain cut-throats in the pay of great men started to shout, "Let the Duke rule for life! Let the Duke be our Lord!" '

They carried him shoulder-high to the Signoria where the crowd threatened to break the doors down if they were not opened and then, having got their way, they installed him in place of the priors who were lodged 'most vilely in the arms-room' and two days later moved out altogether.

At the outset it seemed as though Walter might be acceptable to all the various, conflicting elements in the city. But as soon as he had established his position things changed rapidly. His policy was calculatedly demagogical and at the same time viciously cruel. He elevated an oxen-driver to the priorship and had him dressed magnificently in scarlet.

'But as, on coming out of office, this rude fellow spoke heedlessly of a tax which had been imposed on him the Duke had his tongue ripped out as far as his wind-pipe, and then in derision made him walk throughout the city with his tongue going ahead of him stuck on a lance.'

The Duke became a compulsory idol. 'At almost every corner and on every building his crest was painted by the citizens, partly because they hoped to enjoy his benevolence, but also because they were afraid of him,' wrote Villani. When he emerged from the Signoria, surrounded by armed guards, cheers of 'Long live his lordship!' rang through the streets.

He started a reign of bread and circuses, reviving old Florentine feasts that had fallen into disuse and inventing new ones.

The French style of his clothing was imitated by the fawning and the foolish. 'The young men wore a very tight, short skirt which couldn't be put on without assistance, and a hood with a cowl which went down to the belt and below.' They also wore pointed beards like his 'to show themselves fiercer in arms'.

But behind all this was the most savage regime of terror Florence had ever known. Trials were held in secret, the prisons were so full that new ones had to be brought into service, and capital executions became daily events. He arraigned the chiefs of some of the city's leading families — including the already powerful Medici — and had them beheaded on corruption charges.

Then, as always when the government was entrusted to outsiders, there was a financial price to pay, too, and the purse was still an extremely sensitive part of the body politic. 'In the ten months and eighteen days that he reigned as lord,' said Villani, 'there came into his hands, what with taxes, rates, loans and fines and other means, approximately 400,000 gold florins.'

Boccaccio watched with disgust. Of Walter he wrote, 'He began to frequent the company of flatterers, to give his favours to pimps, to consort with the most debased of people, to impose crushing taxes, to annex and confiscate without pity, without regard for anybody. And for all these things the unhappy citizens began bitterly to regret their lost and so little appreciated liberty, blaming their own folly. Their sons and daughters, their sisters and wives were dragged to the satisfaction of his lusts.'

'Liar!' Boccaccio screamed at him on paper. 'Miser and scoundrel — cruel, inexorable, perfidious, ungrateful!'

Walter of Brienne had a minister called William of Assisi who was notorious for his unbridled savagery. He organised public executions on the lines of popular outdoor festivals and insisted on the children of the condemned sitting in the front row. William succeeded in turning even the dregs of Florence's population against his master.

It could not go on. On the other side of the Alps, King Philip of France, who had a low opinion of Walter of Brienne and also knew his Florentines, is reported to have said, '*Albergé est le pélerin — mais il y a mauvais ostel*.' ('Lodged is the pilgrim —

but evil is his lodging.')

'There is an old proverb which is much to the point among us Florentines,' wrote a chronicler, 'It says: "Florence doesn't bother — until she aches all over." '

Now indeed she ached all over and bothered so much that the whole city seethed with plots. Walter got wind of them and convoked all the leading citizens to a hall 'where the windows were barred with iron', intending to massacre them *en bloc*.

But the leading citizens refused to go. Instead the city rose up against Walter. 'The great ones and the people swore fealty together and kissed one another on the mouth.' The Florentines broke open the prisons and released their inmates before going on to lay siege to the palace inside which Walter had locked himself. But he managed to escape by a secret stairway and somehow got clear of the city.

The thwarted rage of the Florentines vented itself upon the hated William of Assisi. He had tried to escape dressed as a friar, together with his son and, when he was recognised by the mob, he held up a communion host thinking mistakenly it would grant him immunity.

'But God,' said Boccaccio who was there, 'permitted that the said William, whose cruelty had torn so many children from their fathers, should now see his own son cut to pieces before his eyes, after which he, too, was killed.'

He was ripped open like a pig and hanged by his feet. 'And some were so cruel and obsessed with so bestial a fury that they ate the raw flesh.'

18

PLAGUE

The great plague came to Florence in 1348 and almost overnight average life expectancy, which had been thirty-four swooped to seventeen. The symptoms were quite unmistakable. There were swellings under the armpits or in the groin 'which grew to the size of an ordinary apple or an egg, or thereabouts'. These swellings spread over the body. Then black, bruise-like marks appeared on the arms and thighs, and death usually followed about three days after the first symptoms.

Not that plague was unknown to the Florentines. In milder form it visited them practically every year, being brought into the city by travellers and favoured by the appalling lack of hygiene. In winter, rain and the Arno did something to clean the streets and ice served as a disinfectant. But when the weather started to get hot, plague fizzed through the narrow, dirty alley-ways like fire along a fuse, and those who could afford it escaped into the country.

The hospital system that evolved in Florence to deal with this was unique for the period. There were thirty hospitals at which the sick, instead of being laid out by the dozen on wooden boards, like fish on a slab, as they were elsewhere, were provided with individual beds. They were even issued with a knife for eating, a glass and a chamber pot.

These hospitals were run by religious orders, by the guilds and by private individuals. One of the most notable was the hospital of Santa Maria Nuova, founded in 1286 by Beatrice's father, Folco Portinari. The money behind it was his, but the inspiration came from one of the most remarkable Florentines of that period, Beatrice's former nurse, Monna Tessa.

It was she who looked after the sick and then recruited other Florentine women to help her. They became known as the Oblates of Santa Maria Nuova, and the nuns who work in the same hospital today consider themselves as the spiritual descendants of Beatrice's nurse.

But the plague of 1348 was exceptional both for its virulence and its terrifying extent. It is said to have been brought on a ship from the Crimea which docked at Messina, and from there it swept across Europe unchecked as far as Scandinavia.

The most assiduous of the many Florentine chroniclers, Giovanni Villani, set out to report the havoc about him as conscientiously as he had recorded all the other events of the city's history during his lifetime. 'And this pestilence lasted until —— ' he wrote, leaving a blank space for the date of its conclusion.

It was never filled in. The plague snatched him away before he was able to do it. His place was taken by Giovanni Boccaccio who recorded the whole appalling tragedy, without sparing a single macabre detail, and used his report as the framework for one of the most uproariously vivacious masterpieces in the history of literature — *The Decameron*.

The plague, he said, was so contagious that it swept from person to person like a fire 'which catches dry or greasy things when they are close together'. One day he saw two of those pigs which so freely roamed about Florence coming upon the clothes of a plague victim, which had been thrown into the street. And having snuffled them a bit and shaken them in their mouths 'in a very short while, after some contortions, both fell down dead as though they had taken poison'.

'It raged so furiously,' wrote yet another chronicler, 'that in the houses where it struck no one would look after the sick person, and anyone who did look after them died of the same disease. And practically nobody lived beyond the fourth day. And neither medicine nor doctor availed anything.'

Anyway, doctors were practically non-existent — 'because,' as the same chronicler points out matter of factly, 'they died like everybody else. . . . Those that were to be found,' he continued, 'demanded enormous sums before they would even go into a house. And having gone in, they took the sick man's pulse with their face averted, and they would only examine the urine from a distance, at the same time holding some strong-smelling stuff to their nose.

'Son abandoned father, husband wife, wife husband, and brother brother. The entire city had nothing to do but bury its dead.'

As always when some particular peril threatens the public there were voracious schools of thought as to how it could best be avoided. Boccaccio carefully chronicled them all. Some averred that the secret lay in abstinence: 'avoiding all superfluities'. These people removed themselves as far as possible from the general suffering, 'taking the most delicate foods and the finest wines with the utmost moderation', speaking to nobody and refusing to listen to news of death and disease outside their frugal little world.

Others believed that the remedy lay in heavy drinking, delights, singing and the satisfaction of all the appetites, 'and that laughter and derision of all that occurred were the best medicine for such a great ill'. And so they went by day and by night from tavern to tavern, 'drinking beyond all measure and limit'. They were also able to indulge their wildest carnal appetites in private houses abandoned throughout the city and now, to all intents and purposes, public property.

This riotous and often criminal behaviour was made possible because all laws, human and divine, had been abandoned. Those who should have enforced them were 'either dead or sick, or so stripped of their subordinates that they could do nothing'.

There was also a school of thought between these two extremes. The adherents of this school believed in taking what they needed in moderation and, without shutting themselves off from the rest of humanity, they went about, 'some carrying flowers in their hands, some odorous herbs and some divers kinds of spices, often holding these to their noses, believing it an excellent thing to restore the brain with such odours, as the whole air seemed infected with the stink of the corpses and of the sick and their medicines'.

But the paths of abstinence, moderation and excess usually all led in the same direction.

As the sick were abandoned by their nearest and dearest, their only hope lay in the charity of friends — and these, as Boccaccio points out, were few — and the help of servants who demanded exorbitant rates of pay and, in exchange, did little more than 'handing the sick person what he asked for and watching while he died'.

'Many died of hunger because when somebody went to bed sick, the others in his house, who were terrified, said, "I'm going for the doctor;" and quietly they shut the door into the street behind them and returned no more. For nobody or few people would enter a house where somebody was sick, but neither would they receive anybody healthy who came from a house of sickness, saying, "He is infected — do not speak to him." '

Food prices soared, especially sweetmeats and sugar for which the plague victims had a craving. 'Eggs doubled in price, though you were lucky if you could find any, even searching throughout the city.'

Gauze shrouds in which the dead were customarily wrapped in Florence rocketed from three florins to thirty, 'and would have gone up to a hundred if the use of them had not been abandoned altogether in favour of cloth for the rich and sheeting for those who were not'.

'Some escaped to country villas to change air, some to castles. No guild worked in Florence. All shops were barred up, all taverns closed, only apothecaries and churches remained open.'

The thoughts of many Florentines turned to the salvation of their souls. 'Such was the fear that everybody trembled and expected death from day to day.' The churches were crowded with people imploring protection, but as things got worse and they started to avoid each other for fear of contagion, even the churches emptied and some closed altogether. Masses were said in the open at the intersections of streets on small, improvised altars visible from all directions and especially from the windows of the houses.

'It was a sight to see all the people thronging day and night before the judges and notaries to make their wills. The latter of course took advantage of it and demanded enormous sums. Even finding witnesses became very costly. When their services were asked, they demanded, "Is the will already written?" If it was not written, they would not go; if it was written they went, but stayed on the doorstep.'

The flight of friends and relatives gave rise to a strange custom, Boccaccio reported, hitherto unheard of in Florence. Women, however modest by nature, thought nothing of revealing their bodies to male servants, young or otherwise, just as they would have done to another woman, 'which, for those who survived, was perhaps the cause of less honesty in the future'.

Before the plague, death had been rendered more bearable by the presence of neighbours. Women would come in and weep with the dead man's closest relatives while the men collected in front of the house. And then the deceased was borne 'on the shoulders of his peers, with funeral pomp of candles and hymns, to the church he had elected before his death'.

All this was swept away by the plague and, far from being succoured by a throng of compassionate women, the dead as often as not 'passed from this life without witness'. And no longer were they carried solemnly to the grave, but hurried unceremoniously underground in any space that happened to be available. 'The grave diggers who performed these services,' a survivor wrote, 'were so highly paid that many got rich. But,' he added laconically, 'many died.'

Burial with any formality at all was only for the rich. The poor died by thousands, huddled in their homes, or in the streets. Often deaths were only signalled at all by the stink of the bodies which were carried away simply to get rid of it.

Bodies were dragged outside the houses and left outside the front door 'where, in the morning particularly, anybody who happened to be about could see large numbers of them'.

Coffins inevitably ran short and several corpses were often crammed into one, and when they were not to be had at all the bodies were piled up on boards. Frequently when a priest set out to perform a funeral, a queue of deceased stragglers formed up behind him. 'And where the priests thought they had one dead man to bury,' said Boccaccio, 'they found they had seven or eight or sometimes more.'

Then, as the thanatographic explosion grew more violent, they started to dig huge trenches in the churchyards, deep down as far as the water level, and in these 'the newcomers were piled by the hundred, packed in tight one on top of another like goods in a ship's hold, covered lightly with earth, and so on until the trench was full to the top'.

Things were little better in the country. 'The peasants, wretched and destitute, together with their families, without the labour of any doctor or the help of any servant, in the highways and byways, in fields and houses, by day and by night indifferently, died not like men but like beasts.'

And with death scything so indiscriminately about, they abandoned all their usual occupations, so that the oxen and donkeys, the sheep and goats, the pigs and hens and even the dogs roamed the fields, eating the crops. 'And many, as if they had been rational beings, as soon as their appetites were sated by day, returned to their homes by night without the guidance of any herdsman or shepherd.'

'Oh, how many great palaces,' lamented Boccaccio, return-ing to the city, 'how many beautiful houses, how many noble habitations, once filled with servants, with lords and ladies, were now emptied of their occupants, down to the lowest pantry-boy!

'How many gallant men, how many beautiful women, how many comely youths and maidens whom even Galienus, Hippo-crates or Aesculapius would have judged to be hale and fit — how many of these who in the morning ate with their relatives and companions and friends went to dine the coming evening with their ancestors in the other world!'

It was in these ghastly surroundings that Boccaccio started his story. Seven young women met together one Tuesday morn-ing in the church of Santa Maria Novella. They were all aged between eighteen and twenty-eight, 'all wise and of noble blood, beautiful to behold, delicate in their ways and of virtuous comeliness'.

One of them, Pampinea, lamented the life in death they were obliged to lead, in which they heard no conversation around them except, 'The so-and-sos are dead', or 'The such and suches are dying.' If she went home, she said, she found the house deserted, for all her family had been killed by the plague.

'I'm terrified and my hair stands on end. And wherever I go I seem to see the ghosts of those who have gone beyond, and I am filled with fear at the sight of their faces, not as I remember them, but with a most horrible expression come to them from I know not where.'

These seven ladies together with three young men decide to escape to somewhere far removed from all the horror and desolation, and so they leave Florence.

The place they have chosen is 'on a little hill, remote on all sides from our roads, with divers trees and shrubs of a lush greenness delightful to behold'. On top of this hill is 'a villa with a large and delightful courtyard in the middle with loggias and halls and chambers, each beautiful in their kind and gracefully frescoed, with lawns all about and most marvellous gardens, and wells of sparkling water, and cellars full of precious wines befitting both fine drinkers and sober and modest ladies.'

Here they decide to beguile the time by telling stories — one story per day per person — and as there are ten of them, and as their country retreat lasts for ten days, the sum total of stories is a hundred. Boccaccio's title *Decameron* is from the Greek *deka hemerai*, or ten days.

At the end of the tenth story of the tenth day they all retire for the night, and the next morning they return to Florence. 'And the three young men, having left the seven young women in Santa Maria Novella, where they had started from, bade them farewell and addressed themselves to other pleasures while the women, when it seemed time to them, returned to their houses.'

They were only away for ten days, but the plague continued to ravage Florence from March till September. When it finally ended, the population had fallen from 125,000 to 30,000. Nearly 100,000 Florentines had died in it.

Many of the stories told by the young men and ladies in their country retreat had brought blushes to the female cheeks, but they were nothing in comparison with what was now going on all over Florence. After so much death, the city was swamped with a vast tidal wave of carnal appetite. Nature's demand for the creation of new life was so urgent that it seemed as though nobody could disobey it.

'The man who had no wife took one, widows re-married, the young, the old and almost the infants were joined in matrimony.' Even the decrepit were caught up in the frantic universal urge to couple. Men in their nineties married young girls.

'So great was the haste that many people didn't even wait for Sunday to get married.' Monks and nuns threw off their habits,

Plague losses

both literally and metaphorically, and, said Boccaccio, 'giving themselves over to carnal delights, became lascivious and dissolute'.

If the Florentines had been wild and extravagant before the plague, they were considerably more so after it. They were, as one observer put it, 'given over to a viler and more disordered life than before'. Wallowing in idleness, he said, 'they committed the sin of greed most outrageously, frequenting banquets and taverns, gaming, indulging in every kind of wantonness'.

Fashions grew wilder every day. And the women of the people sported themselves in the streets in the dresses of their one-time mistresses who had died in the plague. Many of the survivors refused to go back to their old jobs having, by testament or looting, acquired the wealth of the dead.

But the plague had passed. And before long business was once again as usual.

19

POET

Like the killing at the foot of Mars, the plague was a watershed for the Florentines. Everything that had gone before appeared suddenly distant and blurred by the riot of death that stretched between. And under these circumstances it began to seem as though there might be a case for the posthumous reinstatement of the city's one-time arch-enemy, Dante Alighieri, who had been dead now for nearly thirty years.

That 'most exceedingly vile Florentines' letter rankled less, and the *Comedy* was more topical, more talked about, more read than ever. Could it be, many wondered, that its author's name might after all resound to the greater glory of Florence? Had his banishment been a tactical error? And, granted that this were so, then surely the mortal remains — a source of revenue as well as status — should lie in the city from which they had sprung rather than in Ravenna which had merely been the accidental setting of his death.

A lot of Florentines were beginning to think along these lines, particularly thanks to the pleading of a young fellow citizen who was beginning to be known as a writer himself. Giovanni Boccaccio came of an excellent bourgeois-merchant family; he was said to have lived somewhat dissolutely in Naples, but his background and thinking were unexceptionably Guelf, so there could be no concealed political motivation in his fervent harangues on behalf of Dante.

How could a reconciliation be brought about? Obviously the first thing to do was regain the good will of the family, and as the daughter, Antonia, was now a nun in Ravenna with the name of Sister Beatrice, she seemed to be the person to start with.

And one name immediately suggested itself for the job of go-between, and so ten golden florins were given to 'M. Gio. Bocchaccio so that he may give them to Sister Beatrice, daughter of Dante Alighieri and nun at the convent of Saint Stephen of the Olive at Ravenna.'

It was the first step. The year in which it was taken was 1350, two years after the plague, when Boccaccio was thirty-seven. It was probably this mission which put into his head the idea of writing a biography of Dante in order that the Florentines might become more familiar with the god of his idolatry, for it was at about this time that he started his *Little Treatise in Praise of Dante*.

He was not able to devote himself entirely to it, however, as he was at the same time engaged in another piece of advocacy, also very close to his heart, on behalf of another exiled Florentine. But this time his client was arguably the most distinguished figure in Europe.

As the great plague of 1348 had swept up Europe from Messina, one of its earlier victims, scythed down when it arrived in Avignon, was a nobly born and still young mother of twelve children, Laura de Noves, by marriage Laura de Sade, a remote ancestress of the Marquis.

Before her body had been submitted to the strain of twelve confinements and then totally disfigured by the plague she had been beautiful. (Traditionally she is recognised in a miniature attributed to Simone Martini which shows a modest young woman of delicate features, her golden hair showing beneath an embroidered coif.)

It was at about the time of this portrait that she made the encounter which brought her immortality, though she was never to suspect it. On Good Friday in the year 1327 Laura had attended Mass in the church of Saint Clare in Avignon, and there she was seen and immediately adored, with the same poetical and non-carnal adoration which Dante had bestowed on Beatrice half a century before, by a 23-year-old Florentine named Francesco Petrarch.

If he gave her immortality, she was also the cause of it in him, for it was for Laura that Petrarch wrote his *Canzoniere*. This collection of 207 lyrics written over a period of twenty years was to send his name spinning down the centuries along with hers.

By the time Boccaccio began to urge his reconciliation with the Florentines, Petrarch had come a long way from his humble beginnings in Arezzo — those days when Dante had lodged with his father and so it was said, dandled the infant Petrarch on his knee, for all that must have sounded an uncharacteristic occupation for Dante to be engaged upon. Now Petrarch's was indisputably the most famous name on the European literary scene. He was sought after by kings, invited as guest of honour by the most powerful city states, and his endless journeyings were one long triumphal progress.

Shortly after his birth, his parents had transferred to the father's birthplace, a small village caled Incisa Val d 'Arno, twenty-six kilometres from Florence, and here they stayed peacefully until he was eight when, with that dramatic stirring of hope felt by all the Florentine exiles at the coming of Henry of Luxemburg, they moved to Pisa for the brief, anti-climactic imperial episode.

That done, there being no more hope for them in Italy, they went to Avignon where the papal court was, but as there was no room for them in the little town which was already overflowing with high ecclesiastical dignitaries and diplomats, they settled in Carpentras, twenty kilometres away, where Francesco and his younger brother, Gherardo, enjoyed a pleasant, undemanding country boyhood.

This came to an end when their father sent them to university. Francesco went first to Montpellier and then Bologna, to prepare himself for the family profession of law. But he enjoyed juridical studies no more than Boccaccio did. One should not exercise the legal profession dishonestly, he said later, and one cannot exercise it honestly.

But at Bologna he discovered his true vocation. This university was then the greatest in Europe with something like 10,000 students from all over the known world, and in it Francesco came upon that other vast and magic world of the ancients, his true and lifelong friends and masters, Virgil, Cicero, Seneca. From then on the collection of rare manuscripts was to be one of the dominating passions of his life.

When he was twenty-two, he and his brother were called back to Avignon by the death of their father who left them a respectable patrimony which they quickly frittered away in the high society life of the papal city. With his father gone, there was no longer any obligation to follow the law, so Francesco turned to the Church, taking minor orders, not out of burning fervour certainly (the only fervour that burned in Petrarch was for classical manuscripts) but in order to solve his bread and butter problems.

Good-looking, cultured and witty, he was a natural favourite with the predominantly worldly college of cardinals, and from then on he was never to feel any shortage of ecclesiastical benefits.

The meeting with Laura took place the same year as he returned to Avignon, but love did not prevent him from living well, moving in the brilliant drawing-room society of the city and travelling frequently. He became a dilettante ambassador, executing commissions for his patrons all over Europe.

Wherever he went, Petrarch followed his unerring instinct for running down the right person to establish contact with, and he quickly wove a spider's web of literary and humanistic contacts through Europe with whom he kept in touch by means of a dense barrage of correspondence conducted in Latin.

This correspondence was anything but private. Indeed, his letters circulated among the learned much as the letters of Saint Paul circulated in the early Church. Long before he began to be known as a poet, his name was firmly established in all the major capitals.

As an antidote to the society life of Avignon and the international intellectual set, he bought a house at Vaucluse and dedicated himself to the simple life. He cultivated gardening, kept a dog and even started a fashion for mountaineering, being the first to climb Mont Ventoux with its 2,000-metre peak. But from his country retreat he continued to bombard the world with correspondence in the purest Ciceronian style. He even wrote to the illustrious dead, including Virgil and his other idols.

When he was twenty-seven, at the time when Boccaccio was still an unknown and aspirant poet at the court of Naples, the Parisian senate and the university of Rome simultaneously

offered Petrarch the coveted laurel crown of poetry, the supreme
honour for which Dante had unavailingly sighed. Petrarch
surveyed the two offers with the benignity of a monarch and
chose to go to Rome. But first, he stipulated, he would be
formally examined in public by Giotto's former friend and
patron, Robert of Anjou, the King of Naples and a sort of
unofficial intellectual sovereign of Europe.

Petrarch sailed from Marseilles to Naples and, on arrival,
dedicated to Robert his unfinished Latin poem, 'Africa', on
which he had been working for some years and which had, albeit
prematurely, earned him the title of 'the new Virgil'.

Robert, with his customary fondness for artists, gave him the
sort of triumphant welcome that most courts reserve for royalty,
conducted the examination which is said to have struck with
awe all hearers, bestowed on Petrarch a scarlet mantle and
finally had him escorted all the way to Rome.

The solemn coronation was held in the Campidoglio on
Easter Day 1340 to the triumphant blare of trumpets. When it
was over, Petrarch walked through the city at the head of a long
procession made up of the cream of Roman society to St Peter's
where he laid his laurel crown on the tomb of the apostle. From
then on he was *the* supreme poet, unchallenged and universally
acknowledged.

Perhaps it occurred to him in the secret places of his heart to
doubt his right to the title, to wonder uneasily whether it did
not belong to Dante. Petrarch was the more elegant writer, but
he lacked the divine fire, and he must have known it. There is an
ambiguity in all his writings concerning Dante, an eagerness to
change the subject which betrays an obscure feeling of guilt.

When Laura was swept away by the plague — at exactly the
same hour, Petrarch asserted, of exactly the same day as he had
first seen her in church, just twenty years before — he was in
Italy and escaped it, possibly thanks to the fact that he was
living in Padua where measures taken against contagion were
more stringent than elsewhere. He certainly liked the city,
feeling at home in the intellectual climate of the university
there.

Like Giotto before him, he was struck by the spread of
Averroism there, and he reported having heard several professors affirming that the soul was not immortal and that Christ-

ianity was no more than a superstition of the ignorant. Though no fervent believer himself, he was mildly shocked by this, but above all anxious not to be involved in anything which might bring him into disfavour with his ecclesiastical patrons.

When the plague began to die down, he left Padua to continue his comfortable journeyings from city to city in gentlemanly pursuit of manuscripts and of the famous. Then in 1350 — the year that Boccaccio took the ten golden florins to Sister Beatrice in Ravenna — his thoughts turned towards the city from which his family sprang, Florence.

His visit there was only semi-official for the sentence of banishment on his father was strictly applicable to him as well. Ignoring it, however, he enquired if there were any man of letters in the city who might give him a fitting reception, and on being told of Boccaccio he deigned to accept his hospitality. For Boccaccio, who regarded Petrarch as a quasi-divine being, the world had no greater honour to give.

The man, now awaited with such trepidation and awe in the dark Boccaccio family home, has been described with meticulous detail by himself: 'I have ever been one of the flock,' he wrote, 'a good, but merely mortal man, of origins neither too humble nor too elevated, of ancient family, as Caesar Augustus said of himself. My character is neither bad nor impudent, were it not for repeated bad examples which have spoiled it.

'In youth I was possessed of a body which, though not unduly strong, was extremely agile. I can pride myself on an appearance, not exactly beautiful, but such as could please in the green years of my life. My colouring was vivacious, something between pale and dark. My eyes were lively and their sight excellent for a long time, though it betrayed me beyond all belief in my sixties, to such an extent that reluctant though I was I had to succumb to the help of lenses. My body arrived in an exceedingly healthy state at old age which took possession of it with the usual train of aches and pains.

'I have always had a supreme contempt for riches: not that they did not please me, but because I detested the fatigues and anxieties which are their inevitable consequence.'

Admitting to one great love in his youth, 'unique and pure', he adds, 'I should like to be able to say I was free of lechery, but if I did I should be lying.'

His intelligence, he says, was similar to his body, 'relying on agility rather than strength, so that I have conceived projects with great facility which I have then abandoned because of the difficulty of carrying them out'.

His manner of speaking, according to some, was clear and direct, 'but in my opinion feeble and involved'.

Before the great man had even arrived at the gates of Florence, Boccaccio had sent him an address of welcome in verse which Petrarch was kind enough to judge as 'not ignoble'. Then he arrived and stayed for several days at Boccaccio's house where a firm friendship of opposites began its course.

When he had gone, Boccaccio began to reflect what joy it would bring to him personally, what honour to the Florentines, if Petrarch would settle in their city for good. But to accomplish this the sentence of exile would first have to be revoked. He set about persuading his fellow citizens to revoke it.

His pleading on behalf of Petrarch was received with benevolence. Not only did the Florentines lift the sentence of exile and order restitution of confiscated goods, but they also offered him a chair at their own university.

This university had been founded under dramatic circumstances just thirty years before. At the university of Bologna a group of students had kidnapped and raped a girl. They were caught and the ring-leader, a Spaniard, was summarily beheaded. This infringement of the privileges and protection enjoyed by the university aroused a storm of protest among professors and students, a group of whom immediately transferred from Bologna to Florence where they set up their own university.

Petrarch was obviously the ideal person for the chair of literature. The Florentines began to like the idea. Boccaccio was overjoyed. The only other person whose reaction mattered — Petrarch himself — had not been consulted, a point which everybody overlooked in the general excitement.

In spring of the following year Boccaccio went with the offer to Padua where Petrarch was a lay canon which meant that, although not qualified to say Mass, he was able to collect the stipend. Of his ecclesiastical position in Padua he later said, 'It supplied me with bread and wine, not only for my own support, but with enough left over to sell.'

This stay in Padua was the happiest period of Boccaccio's

maturity. He was able to enjoy in peace the company of his beloved master, to copy the precious manuscripts (which he himself was never able to afford) and even some of Petrarch's own unpublished work.

'And when the day fell slowly towards sunset,' he wrote later to Petrarch, 'we rose together from our work and went into your orchard, already verdant and flowering with newly-arrived spring, conversing together in sweet and peaceful leisure far into the night.'

The only thing they did not converse about sufficiently was the university chair in Florence, for when Boccaccio returned he had to announce that while Petrarch had not declined the offer, he had not exactly accepted it either. And then came the news that Petrarch, a wanderer by nature, had gone off to his home in Vaucluse.

But worse was to come. Two years later it was reported that he had gone to live in Milan, the guest of Giovanni Visconti, Florence's most implacable enemy at the time. And Visconti had given him a delightful residence with a country view near the church of Saint Ambrose.

This was too much for the Florentines. They withdrew their offer of pardon, restitution and a university chair. It was too much for Boccaccio as well. Forgetful of the veneration in which he held Petrarch, he wrote him a letter accusing him of 'great wickedness'. How, he asked, could a poet who had always exalted freedom and honest poverty pass so swiftly to a life of riches under the yoke of a foreign tyrant?

Petrarch replied haughtily that his inmost soul remained free even when he was apparently living under the dominion of a prince. But if one were obliged to choose a master, he added, it was better to live under the sway of a single man, like Visconti, rather than under the domination of an entire population of tyrants, like the Florentines.

Much later he was to sum up the way he really felt about it. 'It seems apparently that I have lived with princes, but in truth it was the princes who lived with me.'

2o

WIDOW

When first it began to circulate — in 1353 immediately after the Petrarch scandal — Boccaccio's *Decameron* caused as much excited comment among the Florentines as Dante's *Comedy*. And they had more in common than seems immediately apparent. Florence itself to begin with, for both works have their roots there and, between them, they give full expression to the mystical, bawdy, fanatical and irreverent soul of the city — the comedy divine and the *comédie humaine*.

They are both colossal architectural structures of the kind that some writers occasionally propose but few complete. The *Comedy* is composed of three *cantiche*, or books — *Hell, Purgatory* and *Paradise* — each ending with the word 'stars' and each containing thirty-three cantos, except for the first which had an additional introductory one, making a grand total of a hundred. In the same way *The Decameron* consists of ten days each containing ten stories, thus also reaching the round figure of a hundred.

Both were written in the vulgar tongue with the express intention of reaching the largest number of readers possible. Both were written for women as well as men, and Boccaccio went out of his way to point out that *The Decameron* was intended to while away the leisure time of females.

Directly addressing himself to this female audience of his, he answered accusations of prolixity by saying that, whereas a concise style was all very well for scholars, it was not at all the thing for women 'who have as much time on your hands as is left over from your amorous delights'.

'Besides which,' he goes on in the same condescending tone,

'since none of you goes to study at Athens or Bologna or Paris, it is only fitting that you should be addressed in more ample terms than are becoming to those who have sharpened their wits with study'. One begins to appreciate why Fiammetta left him.

Finally, *The Decameron* and the *Comedy* both came out in instalments, causing an ever-rising flood of comment and outrage among the Florentines. By the time the third day's stories had begun to circulate, the delight they caused was accompanied by a loud chorus of protest at their bawdry. Boccaccio faced it blandly.

'Who does not know,' he asked his critics, 'that wine which is so excellent a thing for the healthy is harmful for such as are feverish? Yet shall we say for this reason that it is evil? Who does not know that fire is of exceeding great utility and indeed necessary to mortal creatures? And if it then destroys houses and palaces and cities, shall we therefore call it evil?' No words, he says, are ever interpreted healthily by corrupt minds.

Boccaccio could afford to be bland with his critics. In spite of them, or rather with their assistance, *The Decameron* was a triumphant best-seller, and has been ever since. But unhappily for Boccaccio the position of a best-selling author did not bring him the delights he might have hoped for. Since his return from Naples there had indeed been other women. No Fiammettas, but an Emilia here, a Lucia there; they passed the time agreeably, and if they did not bring the supreme rapture, neither did they cause any great torment.

But then, just when Boccaccio was so triumphantly riding the wave of literary success, he fell in love again, simultaneously this time with a young girl and a mature, but still beautiful widow. He rejected the idea of a double courtship, but could not decide which of the two to concentrate on.

For advice he turned to that well-known Florentine eccentric, Antonio Pucci, the bell-ringer, town-crier and poet who had written of Giotto's carvings on the tower. Young girls, replied Pucci, rarely fulfil their promise. 'So I give you this council as father to son/Leave the lily and go for the older one.'

Boccaccio followed his advice and wrote to the widow, but she rejected him. His fame cut no ice with her. He was elderly and putting on weight; besides he was of plebeian origin while she was of the nobility.

Unwisely, Boccaccio pressed his suit with a second letter which the widow promptly passed to her lover who, unlike Boccaccio, was young and rich. He saw to it that the letter went the rounds of Florence, and <u>Boccaccio became a public figure of fun</u>.

He took his revenge in the only way he knew how — with his pen. He wrote a swingeing satire on the entire female sex called <u>*The Crow*</u>: that being a bird which, like love itself, devours first the eyes and then the brain of its prey. ✓

In a dream, he said, he found himself in a dark and terrible forest which may well have been inspired by that other sinister wood in which Dante had wandered lost and desolate before being rescued by Virgil. In this forest of Boccaccio's the souls of men, now transformed into beasts, expiate the follies of love. And here he meets the late husband of his widow.

'At your age?' asks the husband. 'After so many years of study, do you still not understand what love is, what woman is?' And he undertakes to show him. Women, he says, are no more than imperfect animals, torn by the foulest passions. No animal is more unclean, not even the pig. Their real intentions they conceal with lies and hypocrisy. They set cunning traps to catch their men, and when they have caught them, they never cease to torment them for richer clothes and more splendid jewellery.

They hold men in thrall saying how fragile they are, how they fear a little mouse or the wind moving the shutters, but they are ready to climb up onto the roof if a lover is waiting for them there. Moreover, they are incurable gossips, overbearing, and insatiable for money and luxury.

And not content with having these vices themselves, they transmit them to their daughters, teaching them how to catch husbands, receive secret communications from lovers and feign illness so as to banish their husbands from their beds and welcome other men into them.

As for the widow herself, says the husband, she entered his house like a dove and immediately transformed herself into a serpent. Beautiful? Boccaccio should see her first thing in the morning. She is a monster to behold, sweating and stinking like a goat.

Just after this traumatic affair of the widow, Boccaccio received another, more tragic blow. Before rounding the dangerous cape of forty, he had been sufficiently successful with women to father five illegitimate children, and now one of these, a little girl called Violante whom he loved deeply and tenderly, died suddenly at the age of six.

Years later when he was with Petrarch's daughter, Francesca, in Venice, her little girl ran into the garden where they were sitting and instantly awakened all his memories of Violante.

'Your Eletta,' he wrote to Francesca in a letter afterwards 'is the exact image of my little girl — the same smile, the same happy eyes, the movements and gait, the way she holds her little body — even though mine was bigger, being older, five and a half the last time I saw her. I could see no difference except that yours is fair-haired while mine had brown hair.'

He wrote a poem dedicated to Violante in which he describes how she came one day with her brothers and sisters to console him. He tells her of all the agony he suffered on hearing of her death and asks where she has been, who gave her the white dress embroidered with gold that she is wearing and — a little absent-mindedly — who it is that accompanies her.

As for the last question, she answers that she is accompanied by her two little sisters and her brothers. 'All your children,' she clarifies. As for the dress, it is the gift of the Virgin. Then, when she says they must return where they came from, he tells her that he will die of weeping.

'Weeping is useless,' she says. 'Every creature is born to die. What I have already done, you, too, will do one day. I leave you for a brief while, but afterwards you will surely see me again and we shall be happy together for all eternity.'

Where will he be able to find her after his death?

'In a place apart,' she says, 'where sinners cannot climb, where it is always spring, where the sun is gold and the moon silver, where death, age and suffering no longer exist.'

How, he begs her, can he find the wings to soar there?

'Feed the hungry,' she answers, 'give drink to the thirsty, clothe the naked, visit those in prison, succour the wretched. These good works will give you the wings to rise to God.'

It is a far cry from *The Decameron*.

A few months before Violante's death Boccaccio had embarked upon a new activity on behalf of his fellow citizens, accepting the role of Florentine ambassador.

Diplomacy was not a career in those days, but rather a duty which the literate were called upon to perform from time to time for the public good. Nobody had fixed embassies abroad, but ambassadors were sent as the occasion demanded, and when their specific task was done they returned home once more as private citizens.

The job was by no means well paid, and the ambassador had to maintain his own servants and horses. He was not allowed to undertake any private transactions while engaged upon official business, and if the embassy lasted for longer than had been agreed upon he had to pay a fine. The only concession was that if a horse went lame or died during the journey, the republic would reimburse all or part of its value.

If an embassy was of particular importance, the ambassador was sometimes given a mounted escort and the Pisans, ostentatious spendthrifts, even had him accompanied by the sound of trumpets. The Florentines, who knew the value of money, did not run to such extremes.

Boccaccio's mission was a weighty one. Yet another Holy Roman Emperor was coming down to Italy and the Florentines were concerned about it. Not panic-stricken as at the coming of Henry of Luxemburg — times had changed and Ghibellinism was no more than a ghost sporadically raised by the politicians — but by no means indifferent either.

The Emperor in question was Charles IV, Duke of Luxemburg, founder of the university of Prague and connoisseur of fine wines. He was shrewder than Henry and altogether lacking in his idealism.

The Florentines were in two minds about his coming. On the one hand they felt it might call a halt to the overreaching ambition of Giovanni Visconti, Petrarch's deadly host, who was then a threat to the very existence of Florence. On the other, he might interfere with their cherished republican freedom.

Much depended on what the ascetic, would-be reformer Pope, Innocent VI, felt about it. If he were against Charles, the Florentines could openly be so, too, but if he were for him, their opposition would have to be cautious, for loyalty to the Holy See was a constant in Florentine politics when there was nothing to be lost by it.

So Boccaccio — author of *The Decameron*, that merry-go-round of carnal delights in which the clergy are shown as fornicators and greedy-guts — set off for the papal court at Avignon.

He was well received there and his protracted parleys with high-ranking prelates and the Pope himself were a demonstration of his diplomatic skill, and although the forty-five days conceded him expired without sufficient results, instead of imposing a fine, the Florentines gave him a further fifteen days.

The exact result of the embassy is not known, but he must have carried back much valuable information, for the mission was held to be a great success.

Charles did come a few months later. He was crowned in Milan with the imperial crown, now retrieved from pawn, and in Rome with the crown of Italy.

Petrarch, an outrageous political reactionary who had written to Charles formally inviting him into 'the garden of the empire' to restore peace, was overjoyed. Boccaccio and the Florentines were at the same time disgusted and alarmed. But their worst fears were not realised. The Emperor was content with formal recognition of his sway, a vassalage tax of 100,000 florins and revocation of various sentences of banishment issued at the time of his predecessor, Henry.

On the whole the Florentines felt they had got off lightly, and much of the merit was Boccaccio's which more than made up for the Petrarch fiasco.

A year later he received an invitation to Naples which he seized as a drowning man does a rope. Naples always seemed to hold out happiness to him and always, unfailingly, deluded him cruelly when he tried to grasp it.

The person who invited him was yet another Florentine, an old school-friend of Boccaccio's called Nicola Acciaiuoli. As boys they had both gone to Naples at more or less the same time, but once there, their lives had taken different turnings. Boccaccio had headed confidently towards love and literature, Nicola towards high finance and politics.

He became lover-counsellor to the king's ageing sister-in-law, Catherine de Valois-Courtenay, was knighted at twenty-five and, at the time of the invitation, was one of the most powerful men in the kingdom.

Boccaccio set off from Florence with his hopes high, but when he arrived at Nocera near Naples, Nicola's favourite residence, they began to falter. The welcome was cold, the hospitality poor. He was given a bare room, facing north, and obliged to share the wretched, pillow-less bed. The food was disgusting, the wine vinegary and the company low.

Christmas came shortly after Boccaccio's arrival, and Nicola, who had not yet even received his guest, decided to move court to the shores of Lake Lucrino. Boccaccio packed up the trunk-loads of books that accompanied him wherever he went and set off hoping for better things. He was disappointed. Here the room given him was even fouler than the last one, with a bed 'scarcely sufficient for a dog'.

Immediately after Christmas, Nicola and his court returned to Naples, and in the haste of departure Boccaccio was left behind. For two days he stayed there alone, without food or shops, without servants, abandoned on the deserted shores of the lake. At the end of the two days Nicola's servants arrived to pick him up and take him to Naples. But Boccaccio had had enough. He declined the invitation and set off north once again with his heavy load of books.

Shortly after this, he went to stay with Petrarch once more. The quarrel about Petrarch's disloyal acceptance of the Visconti invitation had been patched up, but a new one threatened to explode when Boccaccio discovered that in his friend's house there was no copy of Dante's *Comedy*.

Was it possible that a wealthy bibliophile like Petrarch who spent his life in the pursuit of manuscripts and had, moreover, half a dozen copyists at his service, was it possible that such a man should be without the greatest work of the age? Could it be that Petrarch did not like Dante? Could it even be that he was jealous?

In theory, Petrarch had admitted Dante's pre-eminence in a discussion about their relative positions in the eyes of posterity. This discussion had arisen when Boccaccio, who always considered himself a nonentity in comparison with the other two, read some verses of Petrarch's and, in a fit of self-denigration, destroyed such of his own as were handy.

Informed of this by a mutual friend, Petrarch wrote to Boccaccio in a tone of benign reproval. Had Boccaccio destroyed his verses because he felt they could never reach the grandeur of Petrarch's? There was no need for such extravagance. Let him pacifically accept the *third* place. Or if he really wanted the *second*, why then *Petrarch would relinquish it*.

'I concede it to you gladly,' he wrote, 'but only think how those out in front have to suffer, always the object of criticism and envy. Coming after us, you are left in peace. Why not content yourself with coming immediately after me, and follow in such a way that nobody will be able to place themselves between us?'

In spite of all this benevolence, Boccaccio never dreamed of showing the vulgar *Decameron* to the master. But somehow or other it came into his hands. He glanced condescendingly through the description of the plague at the beginning and then skipped to the last of the hundred stories which is that of the Patient Griselda. It was not altogether despicable, he decided. There was even a certain crude charm about it. So Petrarch set about bestowing the supreme mark of his approval.

He took the hundredth tale and translated it into Latin.

21

COMEDY

The occasion was unique and the Florentines crammed into the church of Saint Stephen for it. There was much gossip and speculation while they waited and then, as an unnaturally flabby, sick-looking man, old beyond his years, climbed wheezily into the pulpit, silence slowly gained control throughout the church. Those who had known him in the past were shocked by his appearance. To them it must have seemed impossible that life should have evolved this bald and ailing scholar from the brilliant young philanderer, Giovanni Boccaccio.

What interested the Florentines, however, was not so much his appearance as what he had to say. It was now nearly a quarter of a century ago that Boccaccio had entered upon his passionate advocacy in the cause of Dante's rehabilitation, and his pleading had done its work. The Florentines, for all the lures of commerce, had never entirely lost sight of God and Poetry, and now they wanted to know more about the *Comedy* which discoursed so sublimely in one about the other.

A petition had been raised in which the signatories said that they were 'desirous for themselves; for their fellow citizens and also for their descendants to be instructed in the book of Dante, from which even the unlettered may learn to flee vice and acquire virtue'.

Humbly they asked for the election of 'a wise and skilful man, well versed in the doctrine of this poem who, for a period of not more than one year, will give lessons concerning the book vulgarly known as 'el Dante' to whoever wishes to come and hear them on all days which are not holidays, for uninterrupted lessons as is usual, with what salary pleases you, not greater than 100 golden florins'.

On 12 August 1373 the government approved the idea with 186 votes in favour and 19 against (and it is difficult not to wonder whether the 19 had relatives or family friends whose presence in Hell had been reported by Dante).

Two weeks later Boccaccio was nominated reader-instructor, no other name of remotely comparable prestige suggesting itself. For all he was tired and ill, the thought of bringing Dante to so many people, coupled with the prospect of 100 golden florins, overcame these handicaps and, difficult though writing had become, he set to work on his commentary with an enthusiasm born of love.

Everybody in the audience at Saint Stephen's on that Sunday 23 October 1373 knew of *The Decameron*, everybody knew of the *Comedy*. Now they were to hear the author of the first reading and commenting the still controversial contents of the second.

They waited expectantly.

It was not surprising the Florentines were shocked by Boccaccio's appearance for they had seen little of him for more than ten years, during which time he had been living at the family house in Certaldo. The cause of his moving there had been another explosion of Florentine politics which had come near to injuring him as an entirely innocent bystander.

By 1358 the minor guilds had gained control of the government which meant in practice that Florence was ruled by a handful of ignorant, demagogical, politically crass union leaders, and they, to retain power and suppress all opposition, raised once again the old spectre of Ghibellinism.

They demanded the suppression of all those who 'with the souls of ravening wolves under the skins of mild lambs are seeking to enter the sheep-fold'. A single denunciation, even made anonymously, would be sufficient for the authorities to proceed, and the accused person would be subject, if lucky to life exclusion from public office, if unlucky to crushing fines and exile. The law authorising this was known euphemistically as 'the law of admonishment'.

The consequent climate of terror was ideal for conspiracy, and in fact a group of wealthy families decided that the moment had come for the overthrow of the popular regime.

The head of the conspiracy was a Medici, Bartolomeo d'Alamanno de' Medici, who offered the lordship of Florence to Egidio Albornoz, a Spanish nobleman, former archbishop of Toledo and, at the time of the offer, governor of Bologna. In return he was asked to hunt out the popular government.

The *coup d'état* should have been made on the last day of 1360, but the conspirators had overlooked or underrated one vital factor: the Florentine government, whatever its other characteristics, was unshakeably Guelf, and so was Albornoz. And in fact he simply informed it of the offer that had been made him.

Reaction was swift. Two of the conspirators were beheaded on the spot, others were exiled.

For Boccaccio the affair was painful if not dangerous. Some of those involved had been close friends of his and he had even dedicated a youthful work to one of the condemned men, saying that 'my verses could not suffice' to praise his virtue. It began to look as though he would be better out of Florence. Anyway, the city now only upset and irritated him. He disliked the excesses of the popular government. He profoundly distrusted the politicians who had been 'removed from the soil, the plough and the spade and elevated to our highest offices'. On the whole, he preferred to have nothing to do with Florence.

'If I have to travel somewhere,' he wrote in a letter, 'I prefer to present myself as coming from Certaldo.' And so to Certaldo he went.

From there he wrote that 'rough clothes and peasant food are beginning to please me'. Indeed, his tone suggests that he was almost wallowing in the simple life. But when his former school fellow, Nicola Acciaiuoli, now Grand Chancellor of the kingdom of Naples, invited him there once more, he was off like an old war-horse at the distant sound of a trumpet call. Naples was the eternal mirage for Boccaccio and he could not resist it even now.

But the disappointment that awaited him there was just as bitter as ever. On his return to the north, he once again visited Petrarch who was now living in Venice.

Petrarch liked Venice where he had gone to escape from another outbreak of plague. 'The only remaining inn of liberty, peace and justice in our days;' he called it, 'a gentleman's only refuge.' Boccaccio, who had less high an opinion of himself, was restless there and anxious to be off again. But a singular episode prevented his leaving.

Into the domains of the Serenissima there rolled an outrageous eccentric called Leonzio Pilato who at once revived one of the great passions of Boccaccio's life. Petrarch, who had put Boccaccio onto him, described him as 'more horrible than a wild beast, and yet more appalling for his hair and beard.'

'Insolently,' continued the master, 'wherever he goes he carries his outlandish ways, his beard, his mantle and his hunger.'

But one factor more than made up for all this in Boccaccio's eyes Leonzio Pilato knew Greek. He was, in fact, half Greek. Triumphantly Boccaccio bore him back home and, for all that he was 'altogether wild and unmannered', gave him free board and lodging. The sacrifice was great, but the reward was greater — no less than the translation of the whole of the *Odyssey* and the *Iliad* into Italian. The labour lasted for three years with Boccaccio, a loving slave of literature, inciting, helping and encouraging while Petrarch made helpful suggestions from afar.

As always, Boccaccio could not resist sharing good things with his fellow Florentines, whatever he may have thought of them. Leonzio was wild, dishevelled, eccentric, unbearably rude and a sufferer from persecution mania, but he knew Greek and such a gift had to be made public. As he had done before with Petrarch, so now, heedless of experience, Boccaccio started an assiduous propaganda campaign to have a new chair — the first chair of Greek in Western Europe — installed at the university, and his *protégé* seated on it.

He was successful. The Florentine reaction to this new faculty, however, was typical. When it was realised that the new language had no practical value and could not be used in diplomatic or commercial relationships with the Orient, there was a clamour for its removal. Boccaccio defended it as fiercely as a lioness her cubs, and in the end it was not the opposition, but the professor himself who put an end to the teaching of Greek in Florence. Leonzio taught for two years and then, without warning, boarded a ship bound for Constantinople.

Apparently he regretted the decision, for shortly afterwards he joined another ship making the return journey, but it was

struck by a thunderbolt during a storm in the Adriatic and he
went down with it.

Once again Boccaccio retreated to Certaldo where he
laboured away at the production of endless tomes in Latin,
towering literary mountains — nine volumes dealing with
famous men; 104 biographies, no less, of famous women ranging
from Eve to Queen Giovanna of Naples; fifteen volumes of
mythology and a ponderous geographical tract.

With these works if at all, he believed, his name would pass
to posterity. It never occurred to him that the trick had been
done once and for all with *The Decameron*, and if it had he would
have been appalled. For Boccaccio had repudiated his masterpiece. When a Neapolitan friend of his proposed showing the
book to his new young bride, he wrote back in horror, warning
him of the folly of such a course.

Another episode which occurred about this time confirmed
him in his mistrust of *The Decameron*. One day a friar called on
him with a disquieting message. A Carthusian monk named
Pietro Petroni, he said, who had recently died in the odour of
sanctity, had warned while on his death bed that Giovanni
Boccaccio must mend his ways and repent of his licentious
writings, for death was near and he was in grievous danger of
Hell-fire.

Now Boccaccio had recently taken minor orders. This unexpected conversion (foreshadowed, perhaps, in the dream of
Violante) was completely sincere and had caused him no little
trouble and anxiety. For his bastardy had appeared to present an
insurmountable obstacle. Illegitimate children were barred
from the priesthood along with epileptics, lunatics, bigamists,
murderers, heretics, apostates, anybody who had struck the
Pope, pronounced a death sentence or carried one out. There
was only one way around it — he had to get a dispensation from
the Pope. And here the excellent impression he had made
during his embassy in Avignon stood him in good stead. He was
granted a full dispensation.

So it was that the author of *The Decameron*, now one of the vast
army of Florentine religious, had every reason to fear the
death-bed warning of Pietro Petroni. He decided at once to
abandon poetry and get rid of all his books. He also wrote to
Petrarch for advice.

Petrarch's reply was a model of worldly, if not of Heavenly wisdom. Who was this Pietro Petroni, he asked, and what was known about him? Boccaccio should be on his guard 'for the art of rendering imposture honourable with the trappings of religion and saintliness is ancient and of exceeding general use'. Besides, Petrarch went on, what was so surprising in the message? Death was at hand for every man and life was fleeting, only acceptable because it led to a better. As for the books, said Petrarch, suddenly practical, if Boccaccio really intended to get rid of them he (Petrarch) would buy them rather than see the library broken up.

Boccaccio was only partially reassured by this, but he was prevented from becoming too introspective about the affair by another summons to act as ambassador for Florence. Once again the mission was to the Pope in Avignon.

Travelling for its own sake had never been among his chief delights, and now at fifty-two, with aches and pains crowding all about him, the prospect of crossing the Alps on horseback must have been a daunting one for Boccaccio, but he was still a Florentine and it had to be faced.

The Pope — now Urban V — wanted to return to Rome. But the French, horrified at the idea of losing the Holy See, had raised every possible objection. Above all, they asked, who would protect him against the predators which threatened in Italy? Certainly not the Florentines who were all words and no deeds as far as the Church was concerned.

Boccaccio's job was to dismantle this malicious propaganda, convince the Pope that the Florentines were ready and willing to defend him and his court, and offer His Holiness five galleys if he went by sea or an escort of 500 knights if he chose to go by land.

The mission was such a triumph for Boccaccio that when the Pope finally made the journey (under Florentine escort) two years later he was charged with delivering the official welcome on behalf of the republic. The return was only temporary, however, the final break with Avignon being made a decade later.

In 1370 came Boccaccio's third and last abortive visit to Naples, and when he returned from it to Certaldo once more he was tired. 'The arc of my years is falling to its close,' he wrote. 'I cannot go back to the first day, and I see the last one approaching.' He was assailed by illnesses, notably scabies which attacked even the fastidious Petrarch. As he scratched furiously day and night, Boccaccio must have thought often of the falsifiers in Dante's Hell desperately rasping and grating at their own skin, 'maddened by the itch that still finds no abating'.

To this in the summer of 1372 was added a cough, high temperature, constipation, a swollen spleen and kidney pains. 'My body is heavy,' he wrote to a friend, 'my tread unsteady, my hands trembling, my face as pale as death. I have no appetite and everything disgusts me. I look like a corpse, and I desire nothing but death. I have lived to the age of sixty, I have seen too much, considerably more than my ancestors. Besides, what more could I hope for even if I lived to twice my present age? To see the mountains fly and the rivers return to their sources?'

That was Boccaccio's state of mind and body when the Florentines invited him to enlighten them concerning the book of Dante. Once again he rose to the challenge.

But for all the high expectancy, the commentary was not a success. Although half a century had passed since Dante's death, a great deal of envy and malice were still lurking in the city. This public reading brought it all to a head. On the one hand, Boccaccio was accused of heresy, on the other of debasing the high art of poetry by exposing it to the common herd. He continued against mounting protests and then, after sixty lessons, gave up.

He had, he confessed, 'vilely abused the Muses' by foolishly revealing their secrets to 'the plebeian dregs', as a result of which Apollo had punished him with a terrible illness, transforming him from a man into a resounding flask, 'not full of wind, but heavy with lead'. This was dropsy — one more on his long list of ailments. And he dismissed the whole project, which had seemed so glorious such a short while before, as 'madness', while the Florentines he had tried to elevate to the exalted spheres of Dante's poetry and thought were 'ungrateful mechanics'.

His friends had to carry him back to Certaldo.

22

SAINT

Five years after the Dante reading the most sombrely menacing cumulus that was known in the spiritual sky of the Middle Ages massed over Florence. The city was placed under a papal interdict. Nowadays the words may be no more than a historical catch-phrase, but then they meant spiritual death. Priests were forbidden to say Mass, thus depriving the Florentines of vital spiritual food. And while engaged couples might postpone their weddings until the political situation changed, families unable to have their babies baptised or their dead given Christian burial could not put things off so easily. An embargo on the goods of the spirit was as effective as an embargo on provisions.

It was going to require all the charismatic zeal of one of the greatest of Italian saints to save the situation. But before her intervention, the affair was put in the less reliable hands of eight spurious saints.

The root cause of the trouble was the anomalous residence of the papal court at Avignon. Because it was there, the papal states in Italy, administered as often as not by corrupt legates, were falling into a state of ever worsening chaos. 'It was as though the lands of the Church were like a dry wall from which it would be enough to take a few stones to bring about the ruin of all.'

As far as the Florentines were concerned, the situation could not have been more propitious, and they started scheming to take as many stones out of the wall as they possibly could.

That same Cardinal Albornoz who had foiled the most recent Florentine *coup d'état* attempt was sent in to halt this predictable reaction and shore up the crumbling wall.

His opening moves were deft and punishing. At the time, Florence was in the grip of a famine, and Albornoz cut off her grain supply. He also secured the services of the brilliant English mercenary commander, John Hawkwood, to conduct the military campaign against the city. (The Florentines called him Acuto, pronounced ah-coo-to, which was the nearest their tongues could get to Hawkwood.)

It was many years since things had looked as bad as this and, recalling past dangers — the lowering Ghibelline peril which had led to Campaldino, the Valois-Donati rape of Florence, the coming of the Emperor Henry — the Florentines wondered if they would once again be able to save themselves from a mortal danger which, as always, they had brought upon themselves.

They immediately elected an emergency government of eight citizens who were nicknamed by popular accord the eight saints.

If they could perform no miracles, the eight at least achieved two *coups* which were quite sufficient to counter Albornoz' opening moves. By offering Hawkwood more than the Cardinal had done, they turned him and his mercenaries against the papal authority. Then they patched up a hasty league against the Church of all the other major Tuscan cities, including the old enemy, Arezzo.

The Pope at the time was Gregory XI, born Pierre Roger de Beaufort and destined to be the last French Pope (to date) to sit on the throne of Peter. He was not a tyrant and was considered by many to be saintly as well as able. If he had been on the spot he might have been able to negotiate peace. But he was in Avignon, a prisoner of his own nation and entirely dependent on the information that reached him from Italy. And there was no disputing the fact that Florence was doing everything in her power to bring about the downfall of the Church's temporal power in the interest of her own aggrandisement. Gregory used the only weapon available to him. He launched the papal interdict.

'In the city and the country about it was today forbidden to sing Mass or to celebrate the Body of Christ for us citizens and peasants,' wrote an anonymous Florentine, 'but we see with the eyes of the heart; and God knows that we are neither Saracens nor pagans, and that on the contrary we are true Christians elected by God. Amen.'

The eight saints responded audaciously to the interdict. They ordered all Florentine priests to baptise, unite in wedlock, bury and say Mass as though nothing had happened. The validity of the sacraments under such circumstances might have been questioned, but the priests were forced to obey as the penalties were of exceptional severity.

It was beginning to look as though the eight saints and the Church were locked in a combat from which one or the other must emerge irreparably damaged when the genuine saint arrived to solve the dilemma.

Catherine was the daughter of a dyer from nearby Siena and had already made herself felt as one of the dominating influences of the century.

At the time of the dispute between the Florentines and the Church she was still only in her twenties. She and a twin sister who died in infancy were the result of the twenty-fourth confinement of their mother who, in the words of Catherine's first biographer, filled the house with sons and daughters 'like a fruitful bee'.

At the age of six, Catherine had a vision of Christ who invited her to follow him. When she was twelve her parents tried to marry her to a young man of Siena. But, considering herself already betrothed to Christ, she cut off all her hair. The mother tried to compel her obedience. 'Your hair will grow again and you'll marry!' she is reported to have said. But Catherine was stubborn, and eventually her parents gave way before her indomitable will.

They may have been the first to do so, but they were by no means the last. Before her short career was ended, popes and kings were to learn what submission to her was like.

Having taken the veil she set to work in the leper hospitals of her city, at the same time striving for the establishment of peace among the warring families of Siena — a fair task when one considers they were no less violent and pugnacious than the Florentines.

But before long the field of her activities widened to take in the whole of Europe. Illiterate, she dictated what soon amounted to a torrent of letters. 'I write in the precious blood of

Jesus,' she said, and in it she addressed her communications to clan chiefs, to the most prominent lawyers of the day, to humble anonymous citizens and to kings and princes, to powerful prelates, and eventually to the Pope himself, whom she called 'gentle Christ on earth'.

Her aims were three, though they were so entwined as to seem one — the reform of the Church ('The great bridge of the world to Paradise') in its worldly head and in its members, the return of the Pope to Rome and the establishment of peace among the conflicting states and nations.

Why did so many of the most powerful, and often the most intransigent figures of the age listen to a dyer's daughter from Siena? The answer seems to be that she was possessed of an irresistible charisma. 'When she spoke,' wrote her first biographer who was also an eye-witness of her life, 'she communicated something by which, in a way beyond all description, the minds of those who heard her were so strongly drawn to good and took such delight in God that every trace of unhappiness disappeared from their hearts. All their private troubles vanished, all their burdens were forgotten, and so great and unusual a tranquillity of mind fell upon them that, amazed within themselves and delighted with the new kind of pleasure they were enjoying, they would think to themselves, "It is good for us to be here. . . . Let us make here three tabernacles." '

The final return of the papal court from Avignon to Rome was one of her most ardent desires, and she was engaged in its encompassment at the time she became involved with the Florentines. 'Up, like a man, Father!' she urged the Pope, 'I tell you you have no need to tremble!'

She also pleaded with him to pardon the Florentines as a father pardons children who have offended him. 'Let your benignity conquer their malice and pride,' she wrote to him. 'Peace, peace, most holy Father!' she cried.

They tried to argue against her that the patrimony of Saint Peter itself was threatened by the Florentines. 'The treasure of the Church is the blood of Christ,' she answered. The Florentines were trying to strip the Church of the cities that rightly belonged to her. 'You,' she answered, 'must first of all gather the lost sheep.'

And finally in an almost peremptory tone she told the Pope,

'God requires that you make peace with Tuscany!'

No more able to resist Catherine than her parents had done when she was a little girl, the Pope decided to send her to Florence as an ambassador of peace.

On her arrival she was given a respectable if somewhat suspicious welcome, and she at once set to work on the establishment of peace. She succeeded in organising a meeting of the heads of the various factions, including the Church and the Florentines and, at almost the same time, she saw the achievement of one of her principal ambitions when the Pope finally returned to Rome to stay there. The holy city had been without a successor to Peter for almost seventy years.

All seemed set fair for Catherine's plans when Gregory suddenly died, throwing everything into confusion once more. A stormy election produced a Neapolitan Pope, Urban VI, but the French cardinals, still smarting from what they considered the unforgivable slight of the papal court being removed from their country, elected their own anti-Pope, Clement VII.

Back in Florence, Catherine succeeded in having ambassadors sent to the new Pope, but her own position in the city was becoming more dangerous day by day. She had been imprudent enough to protest against the iniquitous 'law of admonishment' which had been pushed through by the minor guilds in 1358.

'I, Stefano Maconi,' wrote the friar who was acting as her secretary at the time, 'unworthy Carthusian, was in Florence at that time with Saint Catherine who required me, amongst other things, to denounce the scandal of admonishment, if it were not put a stop to forthwith.'

The ruling Florentines found this meddling in their affairs intolerable, and they set about whipping up public resentment against Catherine, an easy enough task as the Florentines were always ready to turn upon their benefactors. The government were aided in this by an uncomfortably hot summer and the usual outbreak of plague, not so virulent as the great plague of 1348, but sufficiently unpleasant to make people resentful.

They stormed to the house where Catherine was lodged, demanding that she be burned at the stake.

Characteristically, she sent away her little band of defenders and faced the screaming Florentine mob unattended. 'I am Catherine,' she said, walking out to them alone.

Her charisma worked as it always did. The crowd fell back, the screams dropped to murmurs which rumbled into silence, and Catherine had won yet again.

'From this great ill,' she wrote to the Pope, 'no great ill came.' And a month later a treaty of peace was signed between the Florentines and the Church. The eight saints truculently put off their haloes, while Catherine retained hers.

When the excitement had died down the news began to circulate among the Florentines that Giovanni Boccaccio was dead.

The last months had been tormented, hemmed in as he was increasingly by poverty and pain. And to make matters worse he had to have a married couple in the house — his stepbrother Jacopo, with wife and two children. For a militant bachelor in his condition it must have been a foretaste of Purgatory. It was only his good heart which had allowed it in the first place.

(In World War II Boccaccio's house was hit by a bomb. During restoration work a pair of women's shoes, dated to the fourteenth century, came to light. The public imagination wove fantasies about mysterious mistresses, but the reality was more banal: the shoes belonged to his sister-in-law.)

Poverty became acute and in January of 1374 he was obliged to sell a small piece of property he owned in the country. Six months later his health suffered another serious relapse. His sight began to fail this time, and his stomach — hitherto a solitary stronghold of good health in an ailing body — began to give him attacks of acute nausea.

'You would not recognise me any more,' he wrote in a letter, 'the skin of my body, once so plump, is now all wrinkled, my colour gone, lifeless and dim my eye, trembling my legs and hands. . . . Rotting half-dead in idleness, uncertain of myself, I look to God, who alone can command our ills, for health and grace.'

Mental anguish was added to physical when the news came in July that Petrarch had died at his house in Arquà in the Euganean hills outside Padua. Earlier Petrarch had written to Boccaccio: 'I desire that death may take me while I am reading or writing.' He was lucky to the end, for that was exactly what it had done. They found him with his head lying upon an open book as though he were asleep.

In his will Petrarch left Boccaccio fifty golden florins to buy himself a warm winter cloak to wear while studying during the cold winter nights. The thought of this set Boccaccio speculating on the winding up of his own poor affairs, and he went back into Florence once more to make his will in the Church of Saint Felicity there.

'Nothing,' he wrote, 'being more certain than death and nothing more uncertain than the hour of it, and it being necessary to watch, according to the gospel truth, for we know not the day and the hour in which a man will die, the venerable and esteemed Master Giovanni, of the late Boccaccio, of Certaldo of Valdelsa, of the region of Florence, being sound of mind, body and intellect, disposes of his property by means of this present testament, dictated as follows.'

Having recommended his soul to God Almighty and to Blessed Mary, glorious ever Virgin, he showed himself a loyal Florentine to the end by leaving ten florins for the Cathedral, though referring to it, as all his contemporaries still did, by the old name of Santa Reparata instead of the new name of Santa Maria del Fiore. Another ten florins went for the rebuilding of the city walls.

After a couple of other small bequests he came to one which gives a detailed domestic interior of the Middle Ages. The bequest is in favour of a woman who had kept house for him for many years. To her he left 'a bed in which she was used to sleep in the village of Certaldo together with bedstead, mattress, pillow, a small white bedspread for the said bed with a pair of sheets and a bench which usually stood beside the bed; a small walnut table for eating off; two table-cloths.' He also left her a barrel of wine.

When he had made his will he went back to Certaldo for the last time to wait for the end.

As silence closed about him, broken every so often by the ever more distant and quickly hushed cries of his brother's children, he must have reflected much about his past life and, from what we know of Boccaccio's self-effacing humility, his own achievements will have appeared to him small indeed. His great contemporaries had left behind them monuments that would outlast the centuries. Dante and his *Comedy* which everybody now called by Boccaccio's title of *Divine*. Petrarch who had left an imperishable legacy of verse. And ugly Giotto, now long dead, yet continuing to live by means of his Campanile and his frescoes all over Italy. There were lesser names, too — Guido Cavalcanti, Corso Donati, Pope Boniface. . . . For good or evil they would all be recorded in history.

But Boccaccio himself? Not yet in the grave, for all he had more than one foot in it, and already he was forgotten. *The Decameron*? The mere thought of it made him shudder. Fortunately, it was too insubstantial to last. Formed as it was of bawdy anecdotes, legends, wisps of narrative, it would quickly crumble back into anonymity. Like his own body, and better that way by far.

He died on 21 December 1375 and was buried in the Certaldo church of San Jacopo. On his grave were written the words: 'Under this stone lie the ashes and bones of Giovanni. His soul stands before God resplendent with the merits of the sufferings of his mortal life. Boccaccio was his father, Certaldo his home, poetry his love.'

Even on his last journey into eternity he preferred to present himself as coming from Certaldo.

To the more thoughtfully minded among the Florentines, Boccaccio's death was a cause for reflection. For he had been the last great link with their own past. If he had not known Dante personally, he had known those who had. And Dante's beginnings were deep in the old Florence which nobody could any longer imagine, let alone remember. It was a harsher, more austere Florence, untransformed by Giotto, in which the Cathedral — and so much else besides — had not even been started, and the name Ghibelline still meant something.

An age had passed, they will have told one another when the news came from Certaldo. Its politics had become history, its achievements heritage.

And then turning from a past they could not recall to a future they could not foresee, they may have felt the bewilderment of strangers in a strange land. Yet had they but known where to look for it, the future was already there in the past. It was there in a name which was only inconspicuous because it jostled in such a vast crowd of other names.

The name of a family which had been hired to start a riot after the coming of Charles de Valois. The name of a family which had surpassed all others in the orgy of looting which followed that riot, even stealing children's clothes. The name of a family which had provided a leader for the most recent anti-government conspiracy. The name of Medici.

INDEX